WHAT BUSINESS AND COMMUNITY LEADERS ARE SAYING ABOUT *FAILURE AND SUCCESS*

"As a pastor, I am often counseling friends and family in many areas. Finances is always one of the major areas of concern that comes to my office. With the Bible having over 2600 references to stewardship and finances, it clearly has placed a lot of responsibility on the individual to be equipped to steward their finances well. I am personally thankful for a resource like this book to provide further insight into my own stewardship as well as to those that I often counsel."

Chad Hunsberger
Lead Pastor, Colonial Heights

"McAlpin's approach to financial planning begins by taking clients through an in-depth, personal assessment of their current situation, spiritual well-being, and future goals. The result of this exercise helps clients pinpoint what is most important in their lives and serves as a foundation for building a financial plan. Using the introspective appraisal as a starting point, this seasoned investment counselor and minister of personal finance takes clients through his tried-and-proven financial planning and investment process to ensure they reach their financial wellness goals. McAlpin's faith-based method is fresh, satisfying, and self-revelatory."

Walter A. Ruch, III
CEO, LibertyFi, LLC

"Every person deals with money, but every person does not deal with money in a healthy way. That's why Chris McAlpin's new book is a must-have resource on money matters. This book is biblically accurate, educational, and inspirational. It's understandable by the average person. And it's written by a businessman and financial advisor who works with money management on a daily basis. If you're trying to earn a living, put children through college, save for retirement, and handle money in a positive way, you need this book!"

Stan Buckley
Executive Director, But God Ministries

"Making good choices in life quite often comes down to getting good advice, guidance and wisdom which comes from experience. Chris and the team at Sound Financial Strategies have more than 200 years' experience in helping people navigate their finances and they have shared some of their best kept financial strategies for growing and enjoying your wealth in this book. Chris masterfully teaches you that your net worth does not determine your self-worth and he helps you realize that your past failures can be erased by God's grace, mercy, and love. This book will help you realize what really matters in life."

Dave Jesiolowski
CEO, Champion Advisor,
Author of *One Decision Can: Make Better Decisions, Live a Better Life*

"Chris is a great leader, advisor, man of faith and friend. This book provides the reader with an in-depth look at how we think (sometimes irrationally) about money. Chris puts everything into perspective and helps the reader put money and wealth into context. Aligning our wealth with our greater purpose, being good stewards, and dreaming big are life-long lessons found in this book. Thank you, Chris, for taking the time to share your knowledge, personal journey, and wise guidance."

Clint Sorenson, CFA, CMT
Co-Founder of WealthShield, LLC

At the printing of this book, none of the above individuals are current clients of Sound Financial, but are professional and personal acquaintances.

FAILURE & SUCCESS

THE STORY OF MONEY

CHRIS McALPIN

ISBN: 978-1-7335228-1-6

Disclaimer
This book is designed to provide information that the author believes to be accurate on the subject matter it covers. Neither the author nor the publisher is offering individualized advice tailored to any specific portfolio or to any individual's particular needs, or rendering investment advice or other professional services, such as legal or accounting advice. A competent professional should be sought if one needs expert assistance in areas that include investment, legal, or accounting advice. This publication references performance data collected over many time periods, past results do not guarantee future performance. Additionally, performance data, in addition to laws and regulations, change over time, which could change the status of the information in this book. This book solely provides historical data to discuss and illustrate the underlying principles. Additionally, this book is not intended to serve as a basis for any financial decision as a recommendation of specific investment advice or as an offer to sell or purchase any security. Only a prospectus may be used to offer to sell or purchase securities, and a prospectus must be read and considered carefully before investing or spending money. No warranty is made with respect to the accuracy or completeness of the information contained herein, and both the author and the publisher specifically disclaim any responsibility for any liability, loss, or risk, personal or otherwise, which is incurred as a consequence, directly or indirectly of the use and application of any of the contents of this book. In the text that follows, many people's names and identifying characteristics have been changed to protect their identity and privacy.

The author is registered as an Investment Advisor with Sound Financial Strategies, an SEC Registered Investment Advisor and as a Registered Representative, offering securities, through APW Capital, Inc., Member FINRA/SIPC. This book represents the opinions of the author only and is neither endorsed or guaranteed by APW Capital, Inc. The endorsements contained on the preceding pages relate only to the content of this text and are not intended as endorsement of the author as a Financial Advisor or Registered Representative.

Ordering information
For information about ordering call 601-856-3825

Table of Contents

ACKNOWLEDGMENTS

A book like this cannot be written without a great team. The amount of processes covered in a complete financial plan ranges from investment expertise to legal and tax knowledge coupled with the behavioral side of planning. It takes an excellent team to accomplish this whether you are writing about the topic or in financial planning practice. For years, our Sound family has worked together to earn and serve our clients while befriending each other in a way that has made work a family experience. We truly want the best for each other. As Vicki says, you are all precious. My business partners Sammy Dean, Danny Matthews, and Karl Simmons have always supported, encouraged, and mentored me in invaluable ways. My business and mental sparring partner, Joel Holden, always seems to deliver on the crazy ideas that we come up with. Our staff does such a super job. A special thanks to Tonia Ray and Marla Breland for crafting sentences out of my chicken scratch. Thank you to Christine Cole for taking care of extra work while I closed myself up some days to write. Susan and Karen are always ready and willing to pick up slack as well. Thank you all.

A big thank you to Dave Jesiolowski for encouraging, coaching, editing, and listening to my philosophizing and conjecture on days when I should have been putting words on paper. Another big thank you to Clint Sorenson for encouraging me for over a year to write a book before we ever started, then giving invaluable input and research on the investments chapter as well as in practice. Joe McQuaid gave great encouragement and input on the behavioral chapter. Without him, it would not have been written. Both Clint and Joe are remarkable partners. Ralph Yelverton and Philip LeRoux inserted exceptional advice in the legal and tax planning chapters. They especially kept those chapters concise, accurate, and usable without turning those topics into textbooks.

Thank you to my girls, my Christie, Kate, Rachel, and Megan. I am sorry that I had to "work" on some Saturday mornings to write this. You are invaluable to me.

Thank you to my Lord Jesus for forgiving my own failures, removing my own shame, and replacing the idols in my own heart.

Enjoy the book!

NOTE TO OUR READERS

At Sound Financial, our purpose is to help others find their purpose for them to live a fulfilled life. We happen to do this through financial planning.

In twenty-five years as a financial planning firm, we have seen so much good when it comes to money. We have seen life-changing successes and people-changing generosity when clients have used their money to make a difference in the community by donating to make a difference in schools, churches, charities, and nonprofit organizations.

On the other hand, we have also seen heartache and misery caused by failure, greed, and complacency. This disappoints us and motivated us to go on a mission to inspire people to be both profitable and purposeful.

In our communities, money is the barometer for success, the fuel for luxury, and the security blanket for far too many of us. At times, we, too, have succumbed to this.

Don't get us wrong. Money is a wonderful tool. Success and excellence are definitely worth working for. Our nation has the best money system in the world. We have a free economy where anyone can work to succeed and has a real chance to do so.

However, money as a scoreboard becomes a terrible, insidious, and destructive master.

This is the reason for this book.

There is a better way to achieve your dreams, be fulfilled, and reach financial success.

But first, you must know that there is an almighty God who loves you. He designed you and wants the best for you. Yet He will not share space in your heart with money, success, or your dreams. Still, He will bless you in ways that you cannot imagine.

This is the story of money and the real cost of your dreams. It's about failure and forgiveness, shame and righteousness, and how if you will allow God to work in your heart you will be forgiven for your past failures, your shame can be removed from your life, and you can experience peace surrounding your finances.

It's about the heart issues and head issues—the practical how-to steps when it comes to money.

We intend to educate both your mind and your spirit and pray that your life will be blessed.

I have written about some of my own personal experiences and challenges that my family and I have faced. The mistakes that we've made are a part of life. Learning and letting God shape you through those lessons is an important part of becoming who God created you to be. My hope is that you can relate to a few of these stories and it will help you write the next chapter of your life in a way that is fulfilling and rewarding. My prayer is that through the practical and understandable desire to succeed financially, God will work in your life and shape your heart.

PROLOGUE

My career is steeped in striving to do one thing: make money. I was raised by a businessman and pushed to go to college to make good grades to get a good job to make good money.

Couple this with growing up in the poorest state in the richest country in the world. I studied during the stock market's "irrational exuberance" of the '90s and worked as a financial planner in the "lost decade" of the '00s. These experiences created a mixed perspective of hope, realism, and a bit of cynicism within me. My desire to effectively use all the resources available to me grew and it drove me towards success, and at times threatened to rule me. I learned that only through Christ can this change.

The story of money is a dangerously exciting topic. Dangerous because so few pay attention to it and yet it is so tantalizingly prevalent in our lives. Exciting because we all have visions of grandeur with money.

Most of us chase after our dreams without ever considering what price we will pay, how far we are willing to go, and what the end goal looks like. Our dreams then take us places that we never expected— some we hate, others we idolize.

Jesus said in Luke 14:28 (NIV), "*Suppose one of you wants to build a* tower. Won't you first sit down and estimate the cost to see if you have enough money to complete it?"

A good friend of mine likes to say, "No one wants to hear what you have to say unless you're painting a picture of a brighter future."

That's true. We see that all the great teachers throughout history painted a brighter future. In this book, we will also paint a brighter future. However, the route to get there is based in reality, which can be ugly. Yet to have the best future, we must deal with the ugliness. We need to unpack the real issues that are holding us back, decide what to do with those, and deal with some of the hurt, so that we can leave it behind and move on to a brighter future.

In this case a brighter future is:

- Stability in your current financial lifestyle.

- Certainty of reaching realistic financial goals.

- The freedom to dream big, be purposeful, be generous, and be fulfilled financially.

Money can be very powerful. We have seen over time how money can be used in many different areas of our lives. It can do tremendous good in the world as well as cause tremendous destruction. And most of us have experienced both.

Money has the power to evoke emotions few other possessions in our life can. We are going to explore how to deal with the emotional side of money and the solution for restoring your emotional well-being around money. This is what we will refer to in the book as heart issues.

The other side of the coin when dealing with money is the logical, strategic, and tactical side that cannot be ignored if you want to be successful financially. This is what we will refer to as the head issues surrounding money.

Aristotle said that we make decisions in three different ways:

logos, pathos, and ethos. Logos is the logical reasons for doing something, pathos translates to mean "appeals to the emotions" and is the emotional drive behind our actions, and lastly, ethos means "character," which is doing the right thing.

Over the course of this book, we will discuss all three. The emotions surrounding money, the practical steps you must take to become successful financially, and being purposeful when it comes to your money.

A word of warning: If your heart is not right, then everything that you gain will eventually be lost. In other words, if you make money, success, pleasure, or even purpose your ultimate heart's desire, you don't win anything. Even if you die rich, you still die.

These are three important life-changing thoughts for you to consider:

I. If profit, pleasure, and purpose are your highest priorities, they will become meaningless to you.

II. If you take something good and make it ultimate, it will become your master and crush you.

III. Life's not about you.

You have a creator God who loves you and designed you for eternity. The profit in our lives is a gift from Him given in part for our pleasure and even more so to be purposeful.

When we understand this in our guts, we can then focus on the tasks needed to be successful financially. Yet now those tasks are set with a renewed perspective. They are lighter and freer; we walk easier within those. Success and stability are not assured in human terms. But in eternal terms, they take on a new meaning that is still important but for different reasons.

Only then can we achieve financial stability, work towards our goals, dream big, be purposeful, generous, and fulfilled.

PART 1
THE HEART STUFF

CHAPTER 1

MONEY FAILURE

"TOO MANY PEOPLE SPEND MONEY THEY EARNED TO BUY THINGS THEY DON'T
WANT TO IMPRESS PEOPLE THAT THEY DON'T LIKE."

—ROBERT QUILLEN

Have you ever wondered, *Will I have enough money to pay the bills this month?* or *Can I pay for my children's college, wedding, or retire?* If you have, you are not alone. It's not just poor and middle America who find it hard to save for a rainy day or retirement. According to a recent survey by Nielsen Global Consumer Insights, one out of every four families making $150,000 a year or more is living paycheck to paycheck.

The number increases to roughly one out of every three for households earning $50,000 to $100,000 and one of every two for those taking in less than $50,000.

Seventy-eight percent of full-time workers said they live paycheck to paycheck, according to a recent report from CareerBuilder.

So why is this happening? We are about to reveal the true story about money and the real price of your dreams. In this book, at times we will use money and success interchangeably. Because for many of us, money defines our success, fulfills us, and allows us to purchase the stuff that makes us happy. Our environment has taught us to think this way. The great news is that there is an answer. We will walk through it throughout the rest of the book.

Money failure is a topic that we cringe to think about honestly, much less discuss openly. This failure comes in many forms. They are the should-be retirees who spent their savings on elderly parents and children that lost jobs in the Great Recession. The single parent with a good job but not making enough because raising kids costs a ton. The power couple with a bank-breaking lifestyle swimming in debt to keep up appearances.

It's difficult to unpack national statistics. The median household income is $61,000 according to the US Census Bureau and average debt for those households is $134,000 according to NerdWallet. This means the average US family has a negative net worth.

High income, highly skilled, and well-educated earners tend to ignore these stats because they don't think they relate.

Yet I remember a story from early in my career. I worked with ADP, consulting with businesses regarding their payroll and HR needs. An office manager from a large medical office called one Friday frantic about their payroll run. We recognized that payroll was deeply personal, therefore we made this our top priority. In the middle of the solution, I realized that this was the doctors' payroll. I pointed this out, thinking the stress might be relieved a bit. The office manager grew more frantic, saying that many of these doctors live paycheck to paycheck! Imagine that, making $750,000 a year in 2001 and living paycheck to paycheck.

Let's call this what it is: money failure. And if we're being honest, we feel like it defines us for life.

What are some of the causes for this?

- A person living a lifestyle beyond their means.
- Addictions such as substance abuse, shopping, and gambling.
- Poor debt choices compounded by more poor debt choices.
- Bad advice.
- Lack of self-education, self-examination, and reality seeking.
- Information overload and confusion.

Why do people fail with money? There are **emotional reasons** why we do this to ourselves, just as there are **logical reasons** that are both inside and outside of our control.

Emotionally, our **ego** sets up **defenses** that twist reality to defend our mental state. **But it lies to us.**

Our **arrogance** leads us to think that we know what we are doing when we don't, or that we deserve a certain lifestyle. This leads us to an inflated view of success or failure.

We will **repress** the money facts in our life, and move upsetting information, thoughts, and decisions to the side, down the road, or outright hiding them from ourselves.

Next, we will **deny** the facts and **ignore the truth, dismiss** our financial position, problem, or our potential.

Lastly, **fear wrecks our financial direction.** Most of us fear failure in some form. This leads us to **freeze and do nothing,** paralyzing ourselves with analysis, or take the opposite route and act recklessly, taking on any risk. Ironically, some of us fear success as much as failure. This causes us to avoid actions that would make us successful even though we have the talent, skill, or opportunity to do so.

There are **logical reasons** that we all struggle with in regards to money and risk failure.

Let's be honest. On a day-to-day basis, financial planning isn't the most interesting topic. It is easy to avoid, allowing complacency to set in. Therefore, we don't find the time to plan and take action financially. **Over time, this simple omission can lead to significant failure.**

Next, we just don't have enough money to buy all the things that we want. Again, we avoid the topic and hope it all works out. If this is the case, have some courage to **interrogate reality and look at the facts.** By doing this, you will realize a lot about yourself and your financial position, then you can do something about it.

Certainly there are events in life that cause small or significant setbacks to us financially. This doesn't mean that life ends. It just means that **you have to pick up the pieccs and move forward, even if it's in a different direction.**

At the end of each chapter we are going to challenge you to act on something because we know and understand that knowledge and wisdom paired with committed decisions and actions are the most powerful ways to transform your finances into what you want them to be. So set a timer on your phone or watch and answer the following questions in the next five minutes.

Think about it. **Write** about it. **Do** something about it.

Describe your current financial situation below. Be honest. This is private.

List three financial decisions that you regret. This could be things like business deals or relationships that did not work out, overspending, not saving, or purchasing a financial product that was not a good fit for you.

1. ____

____

____

2. ____

____

____

3. ____

____

____

Now list the reasons why you regret these decisions. This could be things like lack of discipline, no plan, not doing enough research in advance, unwilling to listen to others.

1. ____

____

____

2. ____

____

____

3. ____

____

____

List the three best financial decisions you have ever made. This could be things like saving, setting and sticking to a budget, hiring the right advisor, firing the wrong advisor, hiring a good CPA, or investing in something that worked out well for you.

1. ____

____

____

2. ____

____

____

3. ____

____

____

Now list the reasons why you believe they were good decisions. This could be preparation, research, getting an education, etc.

1. ____

____

____

2. ____

____

____

3. ____

____

____

You might have heard about the rule of seventy-two, which is the number seventy-two divided by an annual interest rate will roughly equal the number of years needed to double your money. I want to introduce you to another rule of seventy-two, which states that in order for you to take action on something that you just learned, it is best to do so within seventy-two hours or you most likely will not do it at all. So answer the question below and pull out your calendar and schedule when you will do what you have decided to change.

List one thing **you will** change about your finances in the next seventy-two hours.

____

____

____

____

Now list out at least three reasons why you must change this about your finances.

1. ____

____

____

2. ____

____

____

3. ____

____

____

"In twenty-five years of ministry, I have never heard anyone say, nor sense anyone thinking, 'The end of my life is near, I wish I had more money…' Most are thinking about God and eternity. If this is important enough to be so prevalent at the end of life, shouldn't it be paramount as we live our lives?"

—Dr. Keith Grubbs,
Senior Pastor, Park Place

CHAPTER 2

MONEY SHAME

Have you ever had to break your family's rules? Today, I'm breaking mine around money, secrecy, and shame. In 2006, on my brother Keith's fortieth birthday, he called and said, "Tam, I'm in dire straits. I wouldn't ask unless I had to. Can I borrow $7,500?"

This wasn't the first time he needed quick cash, but this time, his voice frightened me. I had never heard him so beaten down and shameful, and it was on his fortieth birthday. After a few basic questions that we would all ask, I agreed to loan him the money, but under one condition: that as the financial professional in the family, I wanted to meet with him and his wife to see what was really happening ... Weeks later, we met at the local Starbucks, and I started right in with the tough-love budget conversation ... Quickly, my brother and his wife went into a fearsome blame game, and it got messy. I vacillated between therapist and pissed-off sister. I wanted them to be better than this … Two months went by when I received a call … Keith committed suicide …

Tammy Lally tells this heart wrenching story about her family in a TED Talk in August 2018. Quite frankly, she tells this tough story best with truth, love, and courage.

Like Tammy, we all have family stories of how failure with money, in business or in a career, has led to shame that someone never seemed to recover from. At times this can mean life and death and should always be treated with care.

Money shame is intensely personal and deeply painful. It feels as if everyone can see your report card with all Fs. It is mental and spiritual poverty when you are rich.

I also wish that I could break that age-old unwritten family rule and air out some dirty laundry. My hope would be that you would see that everyone has money failures and shame, that it tends to run deep, and it's passed from generation to generation.

The cycle moves from failure to shame to a facade. The facade is that wall of success we build to let everyone see how successful we are. It is our comfort that we believe everyone else thinks we are valuable because we are smart, successful, and make good decisions. This facade is also our wall, our fortress, that we will defend with all of our power—often to the death. We hide behind this wall in fear and shame, paralyzing ourselves.

Worse, we teach this to our children because they also must participate in the facade for that wall to hold. This warps their ideas about money, failure, and shame. Therefore, they continue on with the cycle.

Many different experiences shape us throughout our life. Unmet expectations lead to fear and a scarcity mentality. A loving and safe home creates stability.

Let's be honest. Life is not typically lived in the extremes. Therefore, we can have a loving and stable home but make one bad decision and set a form of this cycle into motion.

For example, as a young man, a buddy of mine and I bought a house to renovate and flip. We were young, cocky, and thought we had the world by the tail. We would soon learn that it was our tail that was caught in a trap.

This was a time when a monkey could make a little money buying and flipping houses. We would prove we were dumber than monkeys. We made every mistake possible. We overpaid for the house, then overworked and overspent for the renovation. If that wasn't enough, we ignored the advice of one of the best realtors in the city. We were total knuckleheads.

My goal was to make enough money to buy an engagement ring for my girlfriend—now wife. It didn't work out that way. At a time when amateurs were flipping houses in a matter of months, we held the house for three years. My wife and I actually moved in. She hated it. I would joke that we would have graduation and engagement parties in our courtyard for our yet-to-be-born children. She didn't think that was funny.

Of course, this eventually worked out and all is well today, but the experience was truly painful. I thought I had the right education, the guts to risk, the brains to make money. Truthfully, I was arrogant, inexperienced, and was learning a lesson.

God used this experience to drive more than one lesson home to me. I remember my prayer at that time was, "Lord, even if the next lesson is more painful than this, can we just move on to the next lesson?"

For a while His answer was a resounding NO. This was a shaming and humbling experience. One that I needed.

As a result of this, my wife and I had a choice. We could stop trying anything new or we could face our mistakes and learn from them. We could have chosen that business ideas like investing and ownership were not for us. That choice could have led us to bitterness towards anyone else's success. But this would have been to cover up our own shame for failing. Or we could take a different route. We could and did choose to learn from the experience, to see how God was shaping us, and try again. We did try again—we started a multi-level marketing business and failed. We did not make one penny of profit. In fact, we lost money. Yet we learned a ton about business systems, how to study ideas, and found a wonderful mentor. Most importantly, these two failures strengthened our marriage rather than tear it down. I believe it is because I faced the fact that I had made some stupid decisions. She supported me. We faced these together and didn't blame each other. God used these failures to teach us, and they did not lead to shame, though I assure you that I battled shame then and still do today.

By the way, we are still amateurs at best when it comes to real estate. Therefore, when we have to make a real estate decision, we search for expert opinions and do our homework. Then we grind it out the best we can.

Here is some news for you: most people feel this way at some point and nearly all of them keep it inside. Some of us are afraid to ask for a raise because we were taught to just be appreciative that we have a job. Others were taught to never try the market because a parent lost money in stocks. More than a few have taken big risks that they didn't understand with money they didn't have, and the crash from that loss touched a deep emotion that has yet to be dealt with. Sometimes, our only mistake was that we tried a great idea at the wrong time and the loss was out of our control.

The most successful among us continually wonder if we are good enough. The biggest failures lose and never try again. Most of us fall somewhere in the middle with a seemingly average job, average house, and average life, ashamed of the average.

But your financial life does not have to be this way. Nothing about you is average! We are all uniquely made in God's own image and are not meant to be failures nor drag shame around with us. We want you to break out of this shame cycle. To have travelled a journey that begins with hope and ends with sadness is not a failure in life unless you choose to erase what needed to be learned.

Think about it. **Write** about it. **Do** something about it.

Take three minutes and write down your knee-jerk answer to these questions.

Does your net worth define your self-worth?

☐ Yes

☐ No

Why do think this is?

What events in your life have caused this?

Do you still carry the shame of past failures?

☐ Yes

☐ No

If you could change anything financially, what would you change?

____

____

____

What's prevented you from changing in the past?

____

____

____

"SHAME IS THE MOST POWERFUL, MASTER EMOTION.
IT'S THE FEAR THAT WE'RE NOT GOOD ENOUGH."

—BRENÉ BROWN

CHAPTER 3
MONEY AS AN IDOL

Look around you. What do you see? If you step back and watched people's actions, what would their lives tell you about their beliefs? What would their lives tell you is most important to them?

Now, look at yourself. If someone looked at your calendar, what would it tell them is most important in your life? If they looked at your bank statement, what story would it tell?

Our poets speak often of this. Tyler Durden in *Fight Club* said, "Advertising has us chasing cars and clothes, working jobs that we hate, to buy 'crap' that we don't need." Well maybe Durden is not considered a poet. He is fictional after all. But William Shakespeare wrote, "Life is but a walking shadow, a poor player, that struts and frets his hour upon the stage, and then is heard no more; it is a tale told by an idiot, full of sound and fury, signifying nothing."

Maybe you don't relate yet. I wouldn't have thought so either until a few years ago.

Like failure and shame, do you really want to analyze your life this way? Are you willing to take different steps to get a different result? Most people don't want to do this. They like the facade. It is comfortable. It protects them. But the facade will betray you. This wall will break down.

I will use myself as example again. Not because I don't have other examples. In fifteen years of advising people, I have plenty of examples. But understandably, many people don't want their story written for all to see. Of course, I know mine most intimately. I was thirty-eight years old when I had my first fight with burnout. Which I hope is my last. I was a husband, father of three, and a partner in a wealth management firm. I didn't have the time, the freedom, nor the inclination to burn out. I didn't think that it would happen to me—at least not yet. I was too busy and too important, or so I thought. Our firm was growing and innovative. I was leading a scary good team. I had all my priorities right too. I truly loved God, enjoyed teaching Sunday school, and led mission trips to adventurous places. Yet "I didn't make enough money…" I told myself that I would give that up for future growth. "I didn't have the toys of other guys…" but I really worked and spent time with my family. "Our house wasn't enough…" yet we were sacrificing for the future. If I spoke honestly, I was arrogant, yet I didn't measure up. I was afraid of failure as I have always been, which made me reckless at times. In a weird way I was vain about not being vain.

I remember praying to God, *If you are ever going to call me into missions, please do it now.* I wanted out! Two of my business partners met with me, uninvited, to ask me if I wanted to go into mission work to feel free. They said, "it would be tough but you are replaceable." Being replaceable made me feel better and a little of the load lifted. Another business partner called me out for not resting and carrying too much of the load. I was missing the real success that we were living in and enjoying it for what it was. My wife, with all of the support possible said, "Figure it out, pray about it, business, missions, whatever, I trust you."

The truth is that I thought I was chasing success for the right reasons. My goal was to grow a successful firm, to help people succeed, to be profitable and purposeful, but it had become an idol. I was on my own throne. My image of success is what I was chasing. Whether I succeeded or failed at that chase, it was going to crush me. In fact, that was the burnout. It was crushing me.

The truth is that many of us chase success for all of the wrong reasons. When we do this, only two things can happen. First, we can succeed. We win, and then it is not enough. So we drive for more success, only to find that success is just a drug in a different form. We are addicted and cannot get enough. Like any addict, we craft ways to get more. With success, we become arrogant and self-righteous because success in this way requires that we have all of the right answers. This happens in any career, any income level, and at any stage in life. Second, we strive hard. We learn, work, innovate, and then fail. This failure defines us, because the success that would have happened is already our identity. Now we identify as a failure. This shames us and becomes our cloak. We slowly break, shrivel, and withdraw from the world around us, even if only on the inside.

Jesus said, "*No one can serve two masters, for either he will hate the one and love the other, or he will be devoted to the one and despise the other. You cannot serve God and money.*" (Matthew 6:24, NIV) This is so often quoted that I am afraid that we miss His meaning. He understood our design better than anyone else possibly could. As my good friend

Jack, a long-time school leader and coach, says, "By age twenty we tend to have decided what work we will do in life, who we will do life with, and what god we will worship." I've always found the "what god we will worship" part insightful. Each of us will worship something. Whatever we worship, we will serve with slave-like devotion. This is in our nature, our original design. Therefore, when we take something good like money, success, or a person and make it something ultimate, it becomes our master. We will worship, slave, and find our identity in what we've made most ultimate. This is when money, success, or a person such as ourselves becomes our religion and occupies the throne of our life.

Have we made success our religion, lifestyle, and report card? And have we made money our scoreboard? Look at Facebook, LinkedIn, or any social media of your choice. What do you see? What are people celebrating? What is most important to them?

Now take some time and be honest with yourself. Will what you are celebrating sustain you? What do you fear losing the most in this life? Is that worth trading your life for? Is that what you are actually trading your life for?

Think about it. **Write** about it. **Do** something about it.

Has money been your master?

☐ Yes

☐ No

Have you mastered your money?

☐ Yes

☐ No

What emotions do you experience on a regular basis that relate to your money?

1. ____

____

____

2. ____

____

____

3. ____

____

____

What's more important to you: memories (experiences) or possessions?

- ☐ Memories

- ☐ Possessions

Write down an example of this in your life.

____

____

____

What, in your opinion, is the real cost of idling money?

____

____

____

"It isn't what you have or who you are or where you are or what you are doing that makes you happy or unhappy. It is what you think about it."

—Dale Carnegie

CHAPTER 4

FORGIVE YOUR FAILURE, REMOVE YOUR SHAME, & REPLACE YOUR IDOLS

"HE HAS REMOVED OUR SINS AS FAR AWAY FROM US AS THE EAST IS FROM THE WEST."

—PSALM 103:12 (TLB)

We have all experienced money failure. As we have discussed, money is often our proxy for success or even happiness. All of us have failed at a new idea, of getting a promotion, or even attempting an idea that we knew we should have. If we only had the courage, the money, or the education, we feel like we could have succeeded. There always seems to be something missing before we need to take that last and best step.

Then we all carry our old regrets and shame around with us. These old decisions that haunt us and embarrass us. If only we could still count the money… We hold a grudge and continue to tell the story about how it should have been different.

When it comes to money and success, can we all agree that some of us are destitute, some are arrogant, and many are just stuck, unfulfilled, or frustrated? It's crazy how many of us can be all of these at once. Can we also agree that the world around us has trained us with bad ideas? Entertainment…media…our peers teach us to love and imitate what is sexy, cool, and rich from our cradle to our grave. Our parents and mentors have taught us bad ideas, even with the best intentions. Is it also fair that we have sought the actions that have led to failure, shame, and a weird sense of worship? We are the ones who actually made the decisions that led to failure and then we hang onto our shame only to find our identity in money and success.

When we try to solve these problems, we see the depth of the issue—the many moving parts—and struggle to get a sense of the solution because, so often, we get tired and give up.

In regular middle Americana, those in the middle class and up are taught to go to school, get good grades, and get a good job. We are taught that we can be anything that we want to be if we put our mind to it. Success and happiness are an American birthright. This teaching fails for many reasons. First, you cannot be anything that you want to be because you are limited by time, opportunity, and skills. You may not have the grades or the money to get into an Ivy League school. You most likely lack the resources and connections to become the president of the United States. And let's be honest. You are probably not big enough, fast enough, nor ferocious enough to play in the NFL. This does not mean that you are stupid, poor, or a failure; you just aren't gifted in these ways.

We are not crafted to be just anything. This mindset will lead us to frustration and possibly away from what we were designed to be.

So what is it about the American birthright of success and happiness? Isn't this what we are taught? Certainly, this feels like a driving force of so much that we do. Success is in our DNA. Our ancestors from all over the world risked so much to join and make America what it is. Success pumps through our veins, our screens, and throughout our conversations. Happiness is our constant theme. Our thought is, *Why else would you want success if not for happiness?* Even the US Constitution states that the Creator has given us "life, liberty, and the pursuit of happiness," which is now an American ethos. This creates an attitude that our own happiness and the happiness of those we love is the purpose of our lives.

This is our big problem. We are warped in our thinking. Our pursuit of success or happiness has become a prevailing theme. Certainly, the United States of America is a God-blessed country in so many ways. But while He has gifted us the opportunity of life, liberty, and the pursuit of happiness, this should not be our focus and purpose. Let's face reality. Are we always successful and happy? Of course not. How would you even define this? Happiness is a moving target, while success is an insatiable master.

Now, if I may, I will introduce you to a different idea.

In terms of failure, shame, success, and happiness, it has often been said that you should forgive yourself and move on. Press forward, get off the mat, and try again. These are good ideas and indicative of a good attitude. We are constantly blessed with new opportunities and should get up, dust ourselves off, and get back in the game. We should forgive ourselves. But these are incomplete ideas. They do not work because they do not work completely. In our hearts, deep inside we know this. We have to forgive ourselves over and over again as memories resurface. The same is true with shame, which resurfaces time and again as our memories are refreshed with old events and new challenges. These cannot be dealt with until something more perfect takes their place. The reason that these two—failure and shame—resurface is because **whatever we make ultimate, we find our identity in.** It is that identity we need to shape and polish into perfection. We are wired to worship whatever it is that we make ultimate in our lives. We will serve this idol as it becomes our master.

Therefore, if we have made money, success, or even ourselves most ultimate, we become a slave to that. You will learn money is a vicious master in that it is precisely measured and you can never get enough. Success is fickle in that it is an ambiguous and moving target. You, yourself, are a terrible master in that you know yourself all too well. Because of your failure and shame, you don't want yourself as a master. Yet we are all attempting this.

Yet, a different, timeless, and complete idea—in fact a most complete truth—is for you to recognize that you were not created by yourself for yourself, but by the Creator God who loves you for Himself. This Creator designed you in a better way with success, joy, and fulfillment in mind. He will forgive those money failures and debacles in your life. When He forgives you, only then can you truly forgive yourself. The shame that you feel when you don't measure up and your identity becomes shattered, will be replaced with His righteousness. When you're seen as righteous by the God of the Universe, no other opinion matters. He will remove the ultimate position that you have given to success and riches from the throne of your life and replace it with Himself. This awesome God, your designer, loves you deeply.

This is astounding, amazing grace that is offered to you. You no longer are required to be the hero because He is. God forgives your failures, so forgive yourself. God credits you with success. So the world's definition, even your own, is nothing in comparison. This is great news. He will see you as a success. You will receive freedom to live fully, profitably, and purposefully.

So many struggle to agree with this. God does this through Jesus Christ. This is a free gift to you, but it was not free for Him. In the book of Romans, it is written like this: "*So now there is no condemnation for those who belong to Christ Jesus.*" You are not the hero. Jesus is. You are not on the throne in your life. Jesus is. This is the best news because your way does not work. You are not capable of carrying these failures and shame for yourself. Nor are you capable of carrying success. But Jesus is. Once He is your hero, then you can walk freely, profitably, and purposefully as you live life following Him.

Think about it. **Write** about it. **Do** something about it.

Maybe you disagree with me, so ask yourself: Is your way of success working for you?

☐ Yes

☐ No

If you could change that would you?

☐ Yes

☐ No

What exactly would you change?

____

____

____

____

What's stopping you?

____

____

____

____

Maybe you agree with me, but are struggling. What are you struggling with?

____

____

____

____

In Christ, you are forgiven. *"There is therefore now no condemnation for those who are in Christ Jesus."* Romans 8:1 (ESV). If God will forgive your sins against Him, He will most certainly forgive your money failures that may or may not be a sin against Him.

In Christ, you are declared righteous *"in the presence of the God in whom he believed, who gives life to the dead and calls into existence the things that do not exist … That is why his faith was 'counted to him as righteousness.' But the words 'it was counted to him' were not written for his sake alone, but for ours also. It will be counted to us who believe in him who raised from the dead Jesus our Lord."* Romans 4:17, 22–24 (ESV)

What else are your struggling with?

____

____

____

____

If you could change that, would you?

____

____

____

____

What exactly would you change?

What's stopping you?

"Grace means that your mistakes serve a purpose now instead of serving shame."

—Mike Rusch

PART 2
THE HEAD STUFF

CHAPTER 5

WHY DO WE DO WHAT WE DO?

Earlier in the book, we promised that after spending time on the heart issues involving money and life that we would pivot to the head issues—the practical actions. If you need to, breathe a sigh of relief. We are finished discussing heart issues, emotions, and regenerating old stories that make you squirm. It can be uncomfortable, but it was for the best.

In our first move eighteen inches north from our heart to our head, ask yourself, "Why do I do the things that I do?"

Think about this story. A young husband and his wife were in their kitchen. The young man was sitting at the kitchen table scrolling through the news while his wife was preparing a ham for dinner. The husband watched the wife cut off a few inches from either end of the ham. He asked why she cut the ends off, proclaiming "That's a waste of good ham!" She answered, "That's the way my mom prepared the ham." The husband asked, "Why did your mom cut the ends off?" The wife didn't know.

Later, the wife called her mom to find out why she cut the ends of the ham off. Her mom said, "Because that was the way my mom prepared ham."

The young lady's grandma passed away several years earlier, but her grandpa was still alive. She called her grandpa and asked, "Grandpa, why did Grandma cut the ends off the ham?" He was silent as he thought for a moment. Then he replied, "So the ham could fit in the baking pan."

So many of our preconceived ideas come from our childhood experiences, the environment around us, and our friends and family. Our financial behavior is so important to the rest of our lives. We work so hard, spend so much time earning money, and, as discussed throughout the book to this point, we endure so much stress regarding money. Yet the average person does so little about this. In 2014, the Teachers Insurance and Annuity Association of America (TIAA) conducted a survey[1] that determined that people spent more time choosing a restaurant, a flat screen TV, or a tablet than investment planning for their retirement. What does this say about our thinking? Does this mean that we don't want to retire? Does this mean that we don't care about our money?

Our experiences with people in financial planning settings would declare this is a resounding NO. We do care about retirement. We do care about our money. We simply do not think well about our money. Therefore, we do not behave well when it comes to money, which leads to poor outcomes. This becomes a negative feedback loop in which we have poor expectations and poor actions that leads to poor results, which supports our poor expectations.

So let's start from the beginning. Why does our thought-life matter? We have found that many people ignore their natural giftedness and intelligence when it comes to money, specifically financial planning. The average person tends to follow the crowd, listen to the news, and hope it all works out. They tend to respect their friend's advice more than a professional's advice—many times to their own detriment.

Our thoughts lead to our behaviors and actions. These are too often shaped by our past experiences. For example, maybe your parents lost money on Black Monday in 1987. It hurt your father's pride and wallet. He swore to never invest in stocks again. Then he angrily told you that only a fool invests in the stock market. This shaped your thoughts and eventually your actions. Since only a fool gambles in the stock market and you are no fool, you've never even invested in your 401(k). And your actions were confirmed when all your "foolish" friends lost money in 2008. Your hypothetical father probably never intended for his statement to be taken as fact for the rest of your life. Yet one statement from a parent, in anger and off the cuff, can shape a child's thoughts and actions far into adulthood.

I have a real-life example. A wonderful client of mine has always wanted ultra-low risk, near guaranteed investments, resulting in low returns. This is because her father only retired with his company pension and stock dividends. "Daddy always said…" This lady loves and respects her father. As a financial advisor and friend, I am certainly never going to replace this relationship, nor would I ever attempt to. Therefore, we planned her retirement fully within the constraints she chose. Later, I met her father. I told him how much his daughter loved and respected him, and that she would never agree to any advice of mine that contradicted anything that he had ever told her. He chuckled and said, "She should have listened to you. I'm not always right." This lady used generation-old advice to solve a current problem because "Daddy said…" The opposite is also true. Great positive outcomes can come from mentoring and teaching. She was a great saver, manager of debt, and personal financial planner because "Daddy said so…" Therefore, she has a great retirement in action today, regardless of the low returns.

Our thoughts and behaviors lead us to operationalize a financial plan whether we want to or not. We either think, plan, and take definitive action, or follow the crowd, make a gut call, and gamble on the outcome. Let's think about some examples.

For instance, in 2010 we had politically conservative clients that had just endured the 2008–09 market wreck. They did not like the nation's political environment, and were staunchly opposed to the president. The overall sentiment of these clients was to be conservative. They felt that the country was going in the wrong direction and their conservative values set them squarely against some of the political events taking place. However, the market went up. Their portfolios grew. Yes, it was a rocky ride. The summers of '10 and '11 were terrible. There was plenty of bad news to behold. The crowd, especially the conservative crowd, said to be scared and be conservative. In 2016, the political landscape reversed. Our more politically liberal clients felt the same way as their conservative friends a few years earlier. They also felt like the country was going in the wrong direction, opposed the president, and were sure the stock market would fall apart. In both cases, these intelligent grown adults have every right to their thoughts and opinions. However, economic data and the market data pointed to the stock market going up. And that is exactly what happened.

In other cases, we have had clients want to invest in a particular stock because of something they read on a news site. This stock has a new technology that will change the industry, or it's a wonder drug in the third stage of FDA approval, or some other data point that makes it sizzle. In most cases, I have heard the client say something like, "I missed out on the last stock that my gut said to buy…" In other words, they had an idea to buy a particular stock in the past that eventually went up and they felt like they missed out on making a profit. Therefore, to ensure they don't miss out this time, they will buy this stock because their gut instinct is telling them to. The problem with decisions like this is they are rarely supported by data and have never, in my experience, fit into the client's overall financial plan.

Our feelings and opinions regarding financial planning and investing can lead us astray. We can be wrong and not know it. We create enormous blind spots because we so desperately want our thoughts to be the right ones instead of searching for the right solution. These stories and actions lead to the overall notion that investing in the stock market is more akin to gambling than investing. Far too many people take a gunslinger's mentality to investing and think that the only way to win is to beat the market. It makes a game out of what should be a thoughtful planning process and implementation. Our choices are that we either think, plan, and take definitive action; or we follow the crowd, make a gut call, and gamble on the outcome. The choice is yours.

A relatively new area of study has grown in vogue within the last forty years surrounding behavioral finance. Daniel Kahneman and Amos Tversky produced their Prospect Theory study in 1979. Kaheman won the Nobel Prize in Economics in 2002 and published a book titled *Thinking Fast and Slow* in 2011. In 2017, the Nobel Prize in Economics was awarded to Richard Thaler for his contributions to behavioral economics. These and other scientists are studying what happens in the economy when humans act like humans. These studies are helping us understand ourselves and build financial planning and investment models that will better serve us. Think about it. We can build the best financial plan and investment model for you, but if it does not fit your personality, you probably aren't going to follow it. If you don't follow it, your financial plan fails and you suffer.

A great example of this is a client of ours who years ago told me that he hated his 401(k) and it didn't work. I wondered what he meant and wanted to help him plan for retirement. Therefore, we met and explored a full retirement plan. In the discovery process, I learned that he had been investing money from his bi-weekly payroll into his 401(k), then taking money out to pay for his kids' college, new tires on the family vehicles, and a family vacation. Each time he did this, he paid enormous taxes and penalties. No wonder he hated his 401(k)! Yet this wasn't the 401(k)'s fault. It's not designed to work this way. This intelligent, highly-skilled man was using the wrong tool for the task that he was trying to accomplish. His blind spot was that he thought he was right. Much to his credit, he sought out an education and was able to turn his failure into success.

Allowing our emotions and uneducated opinions to wreck our financial plans is unacceptable. So let's do a better job of understanding ourselves so that we get a better outcome.

Kahneman and Tversky performed a simple experiment to study loss aversion. It is said that they performed this experiment many times over with diverse groups of people. Even today there are numerous examples in behavioral risk questionnaires. The experiment involved asking people if they would accept a bet on a coin flip. If you win, you receive $100. If you lose, you lose $100. Most people won't accept the bet. They then raised the odds. If you win, you get $125 to your $100 risk. Most still said no even though the odds were now strongly in their favor. A few started saying yes when the risk became $150 to $100. More said yes when it was $200 to $100. Most said they would take the bet when it was $250 to $100. The result of the experiment showed that most people need to gain about twice as much as they are willing to lose. **Therefore, the scientists surmised, most people feel losses twice as bad as they feel gains.**

In real life this causes us to make a number of financial mistakes, such as:

- Investing in products with low returns because they feel "safe" while unknowingly risking that your cost of living is going to rise faster than your returns.

- Not selling a stock because you would take a loss, even though the data says this is a bad stock to hold onto. This need to "win" has led many investors to risk much larger losses.

- Not accepting a deal below your baseline, not because it was a bad deal but because you hated the feeling of concession. This person would rather "win" the deal than capture a good opportunity.

- Not willing to be an early adopter out of fear of losing and looking foolish.

- The need to "beat the market." This comes in many forms and hardly ever has anything to do with your financial dreams, goals, or plans.

- Focusing on one investment in a portfolio that has lost money while ignoring the other investments.

- Loss aversion that causes us to not be able to see the difference between a bad decision that led to a bad outcome and a good decision that is currently in a rough spot. It can also cause blind spots to outside forces that have caused a bad outcome.

Our fear of loss, preconceived ideas, and old rules of thumb seem to work out in reality to something like this: We take too little risk when we are young because of inherited ideas and misunderstandings. As we age, we press hard, taking large risks going into retirement. This leads many people to lose at times when they cannot recover from the loss. We then give up because we feel like a failure and take the shame that goes along with it. All of this is a vicious cycle, feeding an appetite for too much risk for too little gain, taking risks to make up for old missed opportunities, or risk seeking because our egos won't allow us to do otherwise.

Now that we have thoroughly beat ourselves up once again, let's search for solutions. After all, that is what this book is about.

Remembering that our self-worth is not determined by our net worth now becomes practical advice in light of how this behavior leads to bad results. You are a professional elsewhere in your life and are fully capable of success. So be ready to apply discipline, thinking, planning, and action.

These are the solutions that we will explore in the rest of the book. First, dream big. How would you define success? What big ideas do you want to work on? Do you want to start a business, ensure your children's success, or start a charity?

A wonderful client of ours spent a career working hard at a utility company. He started young after a few years in the Army. They raised a family and he went back to college while working full time. Life happened. They battled injuries and illnesses. They had a unique goal and stayed focused. Now they're retired and debt free with a nice amount of money in an IRA. Today, they teach GED courses to at-risk adults and write grants for the non-profit they work with. They don't define their wealth by industry standards, and wow, they are successful! This is one excellent example of being both profitable and purposeful in retirement.

Once you spend time dreaming and letting ideas roll around in your head, it's time to set goals. At this time, you should look five to ten or more years out and set a direct course towards goals that will make these dreams happen. You may have to prioritize decisions and accept tradeoffs, especially depending on what age you start.

Your next step is to set targets. Think of these as stepping stones to reach your goals that lead to your dreams. In financial planning, these may be charitable donations, savings and investing amounts, budgeting specifics, or setting steps in a plan. For me with my family, our current specific targets are to set our budget at our current lifestyle of which is a simple style. We are specifically planning for our daughters to go to a Tier 1 university. Then we are making long-term retirement plans that may include more education, downsizing our home, and a cabin in the mountains. For my wife and I, we pray, dream, think, and discuss ideas. We set plans but are not afraid to change as we need to.

A key ingredient to managing your emotions, which is the practical reality of behavioral finance studies, is to know your why. **To know why succeeding financially is important will encourage you and remind you of what is important when times get hard.** Follow your plan with discipline and be dogmatic. Don't be afraid of change or risk, accept both wisely and prudently, and seek a specific outcome. Throughout the remainder of this book, we will discuss how.

Let's get started.

The following is one of the behavioral risk profiling questionnaires from our team at WealthShield. Take this test a little "off the cuff," then turn to the next page to score yourself. Do not be surprised or concerned about your results. We simply want you to learn something about yourself:

RATIONALITY

1. There are water lilies on a lake. Each day, the amount of water lilies doubles. After twenty days, there are so many water lilies that the entire lake is covered. After how many days was half of the lake covered?

2. A racket and a ball cost $1.10 in total. The racket costs $1 more than the ball. How much does the ball cost?

3. There are two hospitals in a city: a small one and a bigger one. In which of them is it more likely for more boys than girls to be born in one day, provided that girls and boys have, on average, the same birth rates?

4. Marc looks at Anne. Anne looks at Simon. Marc is married. Simon is single. Does a married person look at an unmarried person?

5. Five machines produce five plates in five hours. How much time do three machines need for three plates?

"THERE ARE TWO CATALYSTS TO THE FINANCIAL PLAN-NING ENGINE; DISCIPLINED ACTION AND INVESTMENT RESULTS."

—JOEL HOLDEN

ANSWERS

1. After 19 days. A doubling of water lilies each day means that one day before the entire lake is covered, half of it will be covered.

2. The ball is $0.05. Ball ($0.05) + Racket ($1.05) = $1.10

3. The small hospital. A divergence from the average outcome is more likely, the smaller the number of cases.

4. Yes. If Anne is not married, the married Marc will look at her. If Anne is married, she will look at the unmarried Simon.

5. Five hours. The amount of plates per machine remains the same.

If you scored 3 or more correct, then you may be a logical investor. If you scored less than 3 then you may be an emotional investor.

We know adults don't always like being called emotional, but FYI, a lot of members of our team are emotional investors too! You will see why we like rules-based investment models in a few chapters....

We hope you learned something about yourself.

CHAPTER 6

THE GAME PLAN

"LISTEN TO ADVICE AND ACCEPT INSTRUCTION, THAT YOU MAY GAIN WISDOM IN THE FUTURE."

—**PROVERBS 19:20 (ESV)**

Now we are ready to go to work. How do you put this into action? The best way to teach how to reach for your dreams, goals, and targets is to give a live example—a case study—to see how this works in real life. We hope that you will apply this to reaching your dreams.

First, dream big. Self-help books are full of this language because it works. Dreams are healthy, fun, and sustaining. Bruce Wilkinson writes in his book *The Dream Giver*, "The better you understand the journey to your dream and what God is doing in your life, the less likely you are to abandon your dream."

The words for your dreams may sound like this:

- "I want to make a ton of money, to be enormously generous, to give crazy amounts of money away."

- "I want our children to grow wise, strong, kind, and Christ-like, experiencing a fulfilling purpose in life."

- "I want my spouse and I to walk well with God and each other, to be free, to be stable, to enjoy some fun experiences in life."

You may say:

- "I want to start my own business for the freedom to do …"

- "I want to grow our business because we will accomplish …"

- "I want to sell my business and go do …"

Words like these are big, freeing, and paint pictures in our heart and mind.

Goals are the building blocks of dreams. Goal setting is a must in planning, but it can be hard. Therefore, take your dreams and begin to give them substance. The words for goals may sound something like this:

- "For my spouse and I to walk well with each other, to be generous, and to best reach for our future, we need to be financially stable in our current lifestyle."

- "Our goal is to send our children to the best university that fits them, for them to flourish in education, and to have the network and opportunities to work in the career that God leads them into."

- "Our goal is to be financially independent one day, so that we can serve in the areas of life that we are called to serve and enjoy the freedom of not punching a clock."

Targets are a narrowing of your goals into tasks for you to work directly towards. These are stepping stones to goals and dreams. They may sound like this:

- "We will set a budget for our current lifestyle and plan goals for the future raises that we know that we will experience."

- "We will plan for our children to go to a Tier 1 university. As they grow, together we can narrow this to the best choices for them and we will be financially prepared."

- "We will plan for retirement at age sixty-seven and grow our resources to that date. One of us will most likely have a second career, but we will plan for retirement as if we won't."

To aim at these targets, we must be able to both measure where they are today and in the future.

We start with a budget. I know, this sounds painful. However, it's not as bad as you think and it is a very helpful exercise. The key purpose of a budget is to track and plan your income and expenses. Personally, we have done this many different ways over the years. Once, we manually wrote down every penny spent in a pocket notebook. We have often used spreadsheets. Now we use different technology that will aggregate our financial account data into a preset budget tool that works within our financial planning technology. A simple way to start is to aggregate your bank account and credit card data into a budgeting tool. Tag each expenditure into a preset category. Tools like this are free, very inexpensive online, or can be offered by your financial advisor.

A simple way to think about your expenses is to think about what you would need if you were stranded on a desert island. Shelter, food, and water. Clearly, this is over simplified. Yet we can and should make these categories only as complicated as they need to be; charitable giving, savings/investing, housing, groceries, utilities, entertainment, and debt repayment as needed. These categories can be as personalized and as complex as you would like.

Once tagged into a category, feed this data into a budget. Plan and work your budget to the point that you have a lifestyle in which you give generously, save/invest money for your future, pay your debt off, and then live within your income.

Full budgeting really is the proper way of budgeting. My wife, Christie, an accountant and homeschool mom, handles our budget this way. Joel, the COO of our firm, handles our firm's budget this way. But let's be honest, it's hard to keep up with. Therefore, when it is my job to work on the budget, I fall into the budgeting style of lying to myself. No, this is not really lying, but it is a type of simplistic planning whereby you set your priorities, pay those first, and live from the rest.

For example, you want to:

- Tithe to your church and/or give 10% to a charity,

- Invest 10% into your retirement and college plans,

- Save 5% into a savings account,

- Then live from the remaining 75% of your take home income.

Write down your take-home income (net) and subtract 25%. Can you live from the rest? If this answer is *yes* then set up automatic drafts from your account for your savings and investments and write your tithe/charity check immediately with each payroll that you receive. Do this first. No questions asked. Revisit your plan periodically to ensure that you are staying on track. You should know that this is a looser way of budgeting and subject to change. However, it can fit the daily reality of our busy lives.

Next, let's assume that your answer is *no*, you cannot live from 75% of your take-home income:

- Why or why not?

- What can you and should you change financially in your life?

- What's more important: reaching your future goals or meeting today's needs and wants?

Either answer is fine, just be honest and don't back down from that question. Then start backing down your investment and savings goals and modeling those results. Are those changes acceptable today? If so, then put these in place and move forward. Readjust in the future to move you closer to success.

Regarding your tithe/charitable giving, I encourage you and challenge you to give at least 10%. God's Word supports this—in fact He demands it with great blessings promised. For all of us, we are blessed to be in the position of even discussing financial planning, so let's be generous. This is a significant part of being blessed financially—being a blessing to others.

Step two is to target your highest priority. This top target is typically the idea that got you interested in financial planning in the first place. It may even be the reason that you are reading this book. It's possible that paying off your debt is your highest priority. Or maybe it's college planning or retirement. Whatever your highest priority is, a specific plan should be set.

For example, if paying off debt is your highest priority, there are a number of ways to accomplish this. This should be a significant priority. Using debt properly can be a great advantage. Repaying that debt quickly is a part of its wise use. Start with self-examination to know your exact financial position in regards to your debt. How much do you owe, to whom, and when is it due? Be honest with yourself. Your debt won't eat you but it may feel like it. As an old friend and brilliant businessman once said, "Debt can chew on you, but it can't swallow you."

- How much debt do you owe versus the assets that you own? Is this answer positive or negative? You want to work until it's positive and then until your debt is gone or wisely used.

- How much of your income are you paying towards debt? Do you have enough income to pay your debt minimums? Do you have enough to pay extra? Far extra? You must work towards a low debt to income ratio, meaning that less of your income is going to make debt repayments.

- Finally, list your debt from least to greatest. Pay the minimum on each debt. Take all of your extra income that you have set aside to pay on debt and pay that to the first debt on your list. Once that first debt is paid off, move to the second debt on the list, then the third, etc. This is the debt snowball repayment method and it works!

For the purposes of this book, we are not deep diving into the proper uses of debt and the best repayment methods. There are times to wisely use debt, such as when you are buying an asset, especially an income-producing asset. There are times to take from your savings or investments to repay debts, such as when there would be a severe adverse effect of not paying that debt immediately or if the asset was not performing and the trade off was good. Debt repayment is often a high-priority target.

The second target that is most often considered are retirement plans. Therefore, let's explore this topic. Take a moment and picture your retirement. What are you doing? Where are you doing that? What fun are you experiencing? What purposeful activities are you working in?

As you think about retirement, don't be afraid of work. Work is good and healthy. In our firm, we have helped an untold number of people retire in the last twenty-five years. Those that retire the healthiest have plans to be productive in retirement. We are made to be workers and created to be productive. However, you should certainly retire at some point from the daily responsibility of your primary career. So take a moment to ask yourself:

- What do I want to do in retirement?

- How will I have fun and go on an adventure or two?

- How will I be productive, help others, and continue to use my God-given talents? Don't let your skills and years of experience waste on the couch!

- Who will I spend retirement with?

- Where will I spend retirement?

Money and planning is certainly vital in this picture.

- How does my current financial picture look?

- What do I need to make my retirement picture happen?

- What new skills and education do I need to learn, and how do I gain new contacts to fulfill the role that I want in retirement?

What is the missing piece between the first two sets of questions? Don't be afraid of the missing pieces, but craft a way to make those up. How much time and resources do you have to make those up? How much money can you invest towards making this a reality? What trade off do you need to make? Don't be afraid. Be *honest*. Even if you make trade-offs today to get nearer your dreams, you will be much closer to those dreams than you would if you did nothing. Remember, none of this defines who you are as a person. But you should find your identity in Jesus Christ and walk with Him towards these dreams. Success will be greater and failure won't destroy you.

The last target is one that is often debated but is truly important. College planning for children. Currently, student loans are considered a national tragedy. Read that with at least a little sarcasm. College students that are forced to be responsible for their college grow up faster. This is a good thing. They take school more seriously, get better grades, and apply themselves to more opportunities. However, the cost of a university has far exceeded inflation when tuition, books, fees, room, and board are considered. Therefore, how do you plan for this? First, consider what opportunities do you want to provide for your children? What are their hopes and dreams? This is their life. Our job as parents at this stage is to guide, not dictate. Therefore, consider this a vital opportunity to plan with them.

This is one example. Recently as a part of a client's financial plan, he wanted to include college planning. We discussed the value of 529 plans versus a joint investment account for him and his wife. For their plan, the joint investment account was best because of the flexibility of managing the investments. Now it was time to make things happen. He had been saving for years, and now his daughter was fourteen years old and had her own dreams and ideas. The daughter and dad met. At this moment in her life, she really wanted to go to the old East Coast school William and Mary, mainly because she had fallen in love with Colonial Williamsburg as a little girl. Yet she had another school in mind too, Liberty University. They looked up each school and made a list of the pros and cons. They discussed her goals and dreams. Dad asked the age-old question, "What do you want to be when you grow up?" Together they discovered that maybe Liberty fit that answer better. Cost had not even come up yet. They spent time dreaming about the idea first. Then, using financial planning tools and free online research, Dad projected the cost. He realized that if all of his financial plans continued to progress, they could pay approximately two-thirds of the full cost. He could look at his daughter and say, "Baby, I love you and want this opportunity for you. But you have to want it for yourself. For you to go to Liberty and work on these dreams and goals, you have to pay for one-third of the costs. I know that you have no way of understanding how much money this really is today. So Mom and I will help you learn. But now, school and scholarships have a new meaning. Therefore, you remember that your grades matter, community service matters, mission trips matter. All of this matters most because you are serving God and people. Now the added benefit is that they look good on a resume to get a scholarship too." This was a wonderful and ongoing conversation between dad and daughter for them to reach this goal together by starting with targets *today*.

These and other targets lead you to meet your goals. Therefore, your goals are not just wishful thinking but they suddenly have legs to them. Typically, a budget and two targets are a good place to start. However, there is no universal law regarding this, so feel free to work this plan to fit you and your family.

In your process, you will develop many ideas that you want to work on. However, if everything is important, nothing is important. Therefore, prioritize your targets. Once your first set of targets are on track, then plan for income raises. Plan to be more generous, maybe expand your lifestyle a little. I hesitate to say that, so please don't be greedy. Maybe improve your current targets if needed. Then have a second set of targets that need your attention. For example, does your will need updating? Do you need more in-depth estate planning? Do you have the proper insurances? As a part of these targets, maybe take the next step in planned generosity.

This is your plan, therefore think, plan, and work through each step.

This is where a financial planner becomes invaluable. A professional that has your best interest at heart can provide expertise, insight, and access to the tools and skills that you don't have on your own.

One more thing. Relax. You're on your way …

DREAMS

What are your dreams? We all have them at every age. Those inspiring ideas that excite us, even if we don't let the world know. Quickly brainstorm and write down those big inspiring ideas. What will you be, do, and see? Who do you want to experience these dreams with?

____

____

____

____

GOALS

Now think about these dreams, these big ideas. What are specific accomplishments, that if reached, would set you on the path to reaching your dreams? Quickly, but thoughtfully, write down specifics that you want to accomplish. Think big!

____

____

____

____

TARGETS

Now take each goal and write 2–3 steps that you must take to reach that goal. Don't stress if you don't have 2–3 steps for each. However, think about each goal, be prayerful (ask God what He wants for your life; don't treat Him like a genie in the sky!). Be specific.

If you need assistance in calculating these numbers, go to **soundfsg.com or call 877-462-3744** to schedule a free meeting to learn more about the resources available to you to help your reach your financial dreams.

"YOU'RE OFF TO GREAT PLACES! TODAY IS YOUR DAY! YOUR MOUNTAIN IS WAITING, SO... GET ON YOUR WAY!"

—DR. SEUSS, *OH, THE PLACES YOU'LL GO!*

CHAPTER 7

GROWING YOUR MONEY

"THE STOCK MARKET IS FILLED WITH INDIVIDUALS WHO KNOW THE PRICE OF EVERYTHING, BUT THE VALUE OF NOTHING."

—PHILIP FISHER

I distinctly remember an article from early in my career explaining why many stockbrokers were broke. The lesson stuck with me decades later. It was the 1990s, the technology revolution was happening, and the US stock market was exploding. To be cool, important, and to have something to talk about, stockbrokers often touted the hottest stock to invest in. These are the most common examples that I've heard my entire career: "This stock is in its third stage of FDA approval..." or "This company owns the best new patent on a certain technology..." or "Scuttlebutt is that this company will be bought for X price..." The person constantly sharing this news inevitably risked their own money on these hot tips. I am sure occasionally they worked out, but mostly it was disastrous. In over twenty years of being in the financial industry, I have only seen success from this happen once by pure luck.

The problem that most people have with investing and the stock market is that it is sensationalized by generations of books and movies. An overabundance of information is available and most people don't know what to do with it. Then there is a sense that it is possible to get rich quick. All of these are fatal to the average investor because it **obscures their goals and objectives.**

When you risk your hard-earned money, you want a result. This result should help you reach a goal that is tied to a dream. You may not use these exact words, but you probably agree with the logic. You really don't care what the stock market did today unless it affects you. It is the return on an account that is tied to a goal that matters to you.

It is your savings and investing discipline and skill where you demonstrate your ability to work and manage your money. It is in investing where you put your money to work for you. Each dollar becomes an employee following a business plan designed to earn a profit and succeed in reaching a goal.

This is logical. We understand this in a lecture or a book. Yet while most people probably agree with what we have written, they do not act that way. Time and again, even with all of the tools available to the investing public, the average investor stumbles through investing.

Instead, on the investment section of your financial plan, we want you to ask:

What am I trying to accomplish?
How much risk am I willing to take?
What tools are available to me?
What is my investment system to accomplish this?

Because hope is not a strategy, we want your investments following a distinctive investment system that is best for you.

"IN THE UNITED STATES, THE DOW JONES INDUSTRIAL AVERAGE HAS HAD TEN HISTORIC DECLINES OF GREATER THAN 40%. THERE HAVE BEEN THIRTY DECLINES IN EXCESS OF 20%. RISK HAPPENS FASTER AND MORE FREQUENTLY THAN FINANCE THEORY SUGGESTS. IN ORDER TO ACHIEVE BETTER-THAN-AVERAGE MARKET RETURNS, IT IS CRITICAL THAT INVESTORS EMPLOY A SYSTEM THAT MITIGATES THE RISK OF SUFFERING THE ALL-TOO-FREQUENT LARGE DECLINES."

—CLINT SORENSON, WEALTHSHIELD

"A dangerous but common investment idea to follow is that stocks always go up, just pick a good investment and stick with it." I remember at the beginning of the 2008 market crash, a financial advisor stated that she was telling her clients that "if your plan hasn't changed, don't change your plan." This was this stockbroker's way of saying "don't make any investment changes, just ride it out." This was potentially a destructive investment philosophy for the 2007–2009 markets.

Certainly, in the history of the US, the stock and bond markets have gone up over long periods of time. This is exactly what you want to wisely invest in being disciplined within your financial plan. However, there have also been periods of loss—even large losses. These large losses cause damage in two ways. First, there is actual portfolio damage. Large losses hurt your returns. It does not take a chartered financial analyst to know this. But most people don't realize that it takes a greater exponential return to recover from large losses. For example, if your portfolio loses 20%, it takes a gain of 25% to recover those losses. A loss of 50% needs a 100% return to recover. Second, there is psychological damage. As discussed throughout the book, we carry our failure, shame, and the biases these create into other areas of our lives. I have met a number of investors through the years that sold everything and went to cash in during 2008, only to hold this cash for many years. In their portfolio, they took all of the losses, got scared, and sold all their positions at the worst time. Then they held cash in their portfolio, missing out on all of the recovery that started in 2009. Unfortunately, this happens too often.

Before we continue, let's have a quick lesson on bulls, bears, and secular markets. Bull markets are those growing with a positive trend. These historically last approximately four years. Though the current bull market as of the writing of this book has lasted for ten years, some are arguing that it is now over.

Bear markets are those that have lost greater than 20% and are historically shorter, averaging two years in length. The shorter duration does not mean less pain.

A secular market is a long-term market trend, lasting many years or even a decade or more.

Bull and bear markets mix with each other to create a short-term market cycle. For example, in the last ten years, 2009–2018, the S&P 500 had nine positive calendar years and one negative, including stock price changes and dividends. In this time, there were two occasions when the S&P lost more than 19% but less than 20%, then the market recovered quickly. This is an example of a secular bull market, a long up trend in which you want an investment system to keep you invested. In another example, 1999–2008, the S&P 500 recorded four negative calendar year returns and six positives. However, the carnage of the Tech Wreck during 2000–2002 and the Great Recession of 2007–2009 caused a "lost decade" from 1999–2012, depending on how you measure the data. Within this time, there was a positive stock market cycle between 2003–2007. This is an example of a secular bear market.[2]

As you can see from these brief examples, short-term market

cycles mix with long-term trends that can create the irrational exuberance of the late 1990s or the fear and despair of the early 2010s. In both cases, investors' emotions were wrong, causing individual mistakes.

We believe that investors should avoid the large losses while capturing the long-term positive trends. That sounds easy, even silly, when you read it on paper, right? Yet as students of market history, we have found that most bear markets decline in stages, giving ample opportunity for a well-designed system to become defensive.

Warren Buffett was on to something when he stated, **"The first rule of investing is to not lose money. The second is to not forget the first rule."** We know that by cutting the risk of investing in the market, we can live to fight another day. The goal of your investment system should be to earn what the market earns with a lot less risk. As Mark Sellers wrote, **"Focus on the downside and the upside will take care of itself."** An investor must be equipped with the proper tools to be able to play offense or defense when warranted.

How can we do this? Sure, buy low and sell high, right? If it were this easy, everyone would do it. However, it takes a systematic approach and the discipline to follow that approach. Here is an example.

Daniel Kahneman, in his book, *Thinking Fast and Slow*, pointed out several examples of how simple formulas were better at making decisions than we are. The story of Orley Ashenfelter captured our attention. Kahneman tells of how Ashenfelter set out to predict the future value of Bordeaux wines using weather information from the year the wine was made. Ashenfelter created a simple formula that predicts the price of wine by using the following data: the average temperature over the summer, the amount of rain at harvest, and the total rainfall during the previous winter. What is fascinating is that this simple package of facts and a decision-making tree creates an accurate price forecast. Ashenfelter's formula is extremely accurate—the correlation between his predictions and actual prices is above 90%.

Kahneman wrote, "Complexity may work in the odd case, but more often than not it reduces validity." We believe this is the case with financial and investment planning. A simple algorithm or math formula can be used to predict a financial plan's success, much the same as a formula can be used to predict wine prices. A successful financial goal can be predicted based on the following factors: amount of savings, amount of spending, investment results, and inflation. **Armed with these facts, you can have a high degree of predictability in your financial plans.** This is great news. You have the ability to control what you can control and set up excellent systems to manage the rest. Think in these terms. Your saving and spending habits are up to you. Your discipline in sticking to your plan is your responsibility. In fact, we have seen many successful financial plans driven by excellent saving habits coupled with mediocre investments. However, the best financial plans excel at both discipline and intellect.

So then what about investment results and inflation? Inflation, in simple terms, is the increase or decrease in your cost of living. This is completely out of your control and anyone else that you know. You simply must live with it. However, your investment system is something that can be controlled. I am not in any way suggesting that you can control nor exactly predict the markets. The point is that you can have a decision-making process that can deliver investment results over time. Your strategy should be flexible enough to account for market conditions and should be able to position you opportunistically. Whether you are in retirement, nearing retirement, or investing for the distant future, buying and holding the markets will most likely lead to a subpar experience. You need the ability to weather market declines without abandoning your system. To solve for this, we are suggesting that you use a rules-based approach to your investment mix that can keep you engaged in your plan so that you stick with it through good markets and bad. Investment returns are a product of long-term engagement in the markets. You and your advisor should hold each other accountable to ensure that you stay the course.

The following is an example of a rules-based investment portfolio from the investment team for Sound Financial led by Clint Sorenson at WealthShield. This is from his and Robert Leggett's book *Invest to Prosper*. The system that is explained is a trend-following system also known as a momentum model. The goal is to simply buy what is going up and sell what is going down to invest with the overall direction of the market. We are not suggesting that you try to time the market or make a bet on the direction of the market. As Sorenson and Leggett write, "trend following is about maintaining a harmonious relationship with the market."[3]

We used trend-following in order to take advantage of positive herd mentality and avoid negative herd mentality. We alternate between risk-on and risk-off, depending on the price trend of stocks and bonds. Capitalizing on herd mentality allows the investor to gain access to return stream that does not always move in tandem with stocks and bonds. For example, during the time period from 2007 to 2009, the stock market (S&P 500) collapsed over 55 percent. Managed-futures managers or commodity trading advisors (CTAs) showed positive returns. Managed-futures managers are largely trend followers. Consequently, the managed-futures traders were negatively correlated with stocks and provided the ultimate diversification to a traditional portfolio. The time period from 2007 to 2009 is not unique. During several other market declines and reductions in traditional asset classes, trend-following traders demonstrated the ability to take advantage of the scrambling herd and capture impresses games.

Trend-following seems high risk to many investors who still look at risk as volatility. Many trend-trading systems actually have higher volatility than the market. The fact is that volatility is not risk, and "the acceptance of higher risk in a trend-following investment can actually lower the risk of your stock and bond portfolios because when trend-following zigs, typical stock and bond investments zag." Trend following appears to be an elixir for the behavioral ills of investing. Herd mentality, overconfidence, representativeness, anchoring effects, and loss aversion are all dealt with through systematic trend-following, or momentum investing.

We can use simple rules to replicate a strategy that protects during market declines without sacrificing the upside. In our strategy, we use indices (baskets of securities tracking a particular market) to gain exposure because of their relatively low costs and high transparency. To illustrate the effectiveness of trend-following historically, we are going to provide a simple, rules-based tactical allocation system as a model. The rules are as follows:

1. Rank the S&P 500, Russell 2000, and the 10-year treasury bond based on the three-month performance.
2. Pick the strongest index based on the ranking.
3. Run the ranking system each month.

The important information to gather from the historical results is the performance of the tactical strategy during the years when the market declines. The ability to rotate away from the stock market when the price deteriorates allows for better performance when trouble is present. The core tenets of trend-following and momentum investing is the protection of capital. Hence, the tactical strategy would have demonstrated the most significant outperformance during periods in which the overall stock market is experiencing large declines.

The strategy would have performed well during positive stock market environments. The portfolio can be invested in the stock market when the trend is positive and stocks are stronger than bonds. In other words, this simple trend trading system acts as a risk reducer during the down markets without sacrificing profits during up markets.

Our tactical strategy would have done well compared to the S&P 500 since 1972. In the following charts, we illustrate the hypothetical results to better demonstrate the potential benefits of incorporating trend-following. If you had invested $1 million in the S&P 500 in the beginning of 1972, your investment would have grown to over $72 million by the end of 2014. If you had invested your $1 million during the same period using our tactical strategy, it would have grown to over $335 million. Remember that the model can only maximize returns up to what the market earns. The potential outperformance comes from avoiding down markets.

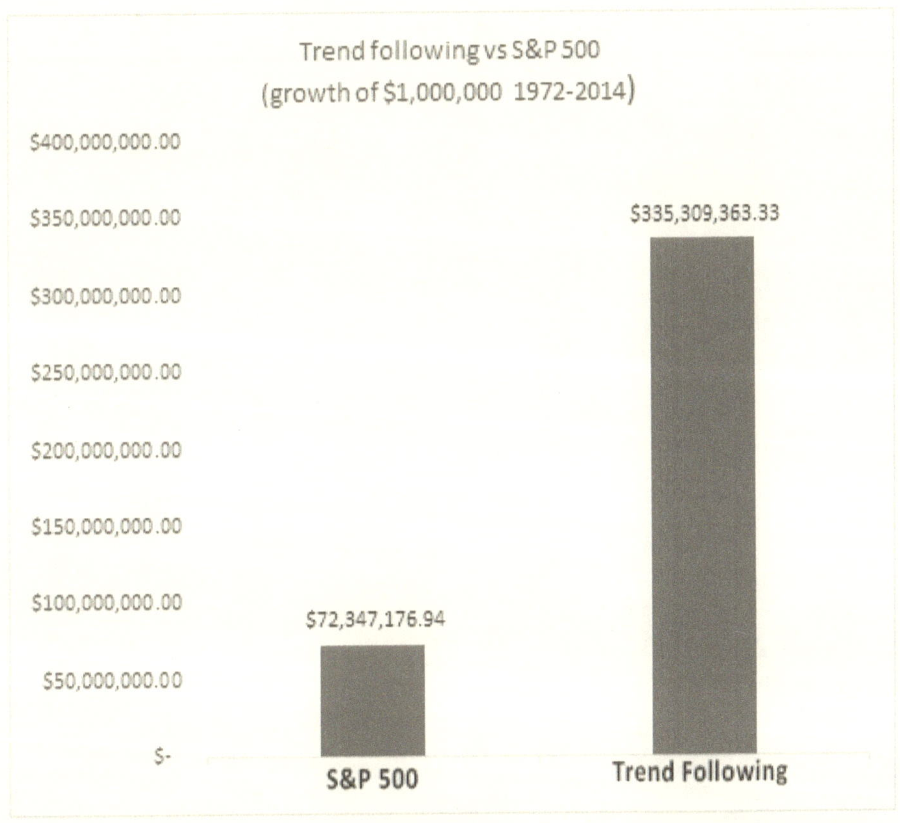

	S&P 500	**Trend following**
1972	18.8%	12.5%
1973	-14.3%	-2.0%
1974	-25.9%	-0.8%
1975	37.0%	37.6%
1976	23.8%	31.5%
1977	-7.0%	3.1%
1978	6.5%	0.7%
1979	18.5%	24.2%

	S&P 500	Trend following
1980	31.7%	22.5%
1981	-4.7%	6.9%
1982	20.4%	46.0%
1983	22.3%	27.8%
1984	6.2%	-2.2%
1985	31.2%	17.2%
1986	18.5%	17.3%
1987	5.8%	5.5%
1988	16.5%	22.3%
1989	31.5%	19.7%
1990	-3.1%	2.4%
1991	30.2%	36.1%
1992	7.5%	13.7%
1993	10.0%	6.6%
1994	1.3%	-4.7%
1995	37.2%	30.0%
1996	22.7%	15.0%
1997	33.1%	37.2%
1998	28.3%	29.1%
1999	20.9%	16.3%
2000	-9.0%	5.1%
2001	-11.9%	-6.4%

	S&P 500	Trend following
2002	-22.0%	-5.8%
2003	28.4%	39.8%
2004	10.7%	12.2%
2005	4.8%	1.3%
2006	15.6%	13.5%
2007	5.5%	-4.7%
2008	-36.6%	14.8%
2009	25.9%	21.1%
2010	14.8%	33.2%
2011	2.1%	17.4%
2012	15.9%	2.5%
2013	32.2%	35.9%
2014	13.5%	8.3%

TREND-FOLLOWING VERSES S&P 500 1972–2014

The tactical system does not avoid declines. Since the end of 1971, there have been nine years in which the S&P 500 declined. Over the past forty years, the trend trading strategy declined seven times (see table 2). The beauty of trend following lies in avoiding the *big* declines. The strategy never suffered a loss of greater than 7% in any given year. In comparison, the market suffered five declines over 10%, of which three were over 20%. Investors must minimize the big declines to succeed when investing. The tactical system is able to accomplish the task of protecting the investors during big market declines, helping the portfolio grow more over the long-term.

As we have outlined previously, trend-following has historically worked to participate in up markets and protect against deep market decline. While we cannot predict the future trajectory of prices, we know that markets will fluctuate, and we have design portfolios to potentially take advantage of market volatility. Trend-following traders have demonstrated their ability to navigate the uncertain markets and capitalize on turmoil. Trend following is reserved not only for Wall Street elite or the ultra-rich. You can apply the same principles to diversify your portfolio using simple index funds.

As you can see, in this case, a trend-following system would have far outperformed the US stock market (S&P 500) during this period of time. Also, this was a significant time period. The 1970s experienced a "lost decade." The 1980s were a significant growth period. In the 1990s, the US experienced the Technology Revolution. Then in the 2000s, we experienced another "lost decade" and the Great Recession. Yet this demonstrated system is a rather simple one using a US large cap stock index, a US small cap stock index, and a US Treasury bond. The point is that it does not have to be complicated to work well. In fact, we want to take what is complex and make it simple so that it is usable. However, it does have to be well thought out, researched, and tested. **The advantage to you is to have a predetermined, tested decision-making process that fits into your financial plans and produces results that lead to your goals.** This removes the guesswork and hope from investing, giving you the best opportunity possible for success.

"The investor's chief problem and even his worst enemy is likely to be himself."

—Benjamin Graham

CHAPTER 8
RISK & RESPONSIBILITY

"EVERY SIGNIFICANT CHOICE WE MAKE IN LIFE COMES WITH SOME UNCERTAINTY."

—DANIEL KAHNEMAN AND AMOS TVERSKY

When it comes to loss, it has been proven over and over again that we will do more to avoid loss than seek gain. We have given examples from stories and studies, and here is another. In a study done by economists Devin G. Pope and Maurice E. Schweitzer in the *American Economic Review*[4], they found that professional golfers—even Tiger Woods—who were a part of this study were averse to loss. The study included data from 239 tournaments completed between 2004 and 2009. In the study, they demonstrated that professional golfers hit birdie putts less accurately than they hit otherwise similar par putts to avoid a bogey. They concluded this is because we are internally motivated more to avoid losses than to achieve gains. In other words, the fear of a bogey was greater than the gain of a birdie.

If this is indeed true, then how should we evaluate risk in our lives? **How we think about risk does not change the probability of the risk happening. But it is how we think about risk, plan for risk, mitigate risk, and accept the risk that matters.** Throughout life we accept risk. Every time you drive on the highway, you accept the risk that the others around you know how to operate the large machinery they are driving alongside you. You are accepting the risk for the health of those involved including yourself, along with your property. Some days this does not feel like a good risk. Yet we drive down the highway anyway. Why? Because we have planned for, trained for, and practiced accepting this risk. Professional golfers have planned, trained, and practiced for the risk and pressure they endure in major golf tournaments in much of the same way. I bet they wished they could insure some of those putts!

In this chapter, we will examine probabilities of certain risks occurring. Then we will discuss the different types of risk transfer and how you can utilize specific strategies to alleviate the feeling of fear related to loss.

When you think about what you can protect in your life, what would you say is most important to you?

Your family and health? Your income and property? Your investments? Or something else? How would you answer for each of these?

Depending on what stage of life you are in, your answer might be different. If you just graduated from college, started a new job, have no family yet, and no home because you are renting, then you might say your health and income are the most important for you to protect. If you are middle aged then you might be more concerned about protecting your family's future, your income, your home, or vehicles. This generally is the stage of life that you have the most to risk, statistically speaking, because peak spending generally occurs in this stage of life around age 46. If you are closer to retirement, you may be more interested in protecting the assets that you have accumulated. During the pre-retirement and retirement stage of life, most people don't want to suffer significant losses because they don't have time to re-accumulate the lost assets.

Whether you are just starting your financial journey or closer to the end of it, it makes sense to examine the risk associated with loss.

Let's do a quick assessment.

Rank the following in order of importance to you currently: 1 being most important and 8 being the least important.

Family   ________

Health   ________

Income   ________

Home   ________

Vehicles   ________

Possessions   ________

Investments   ________

Now that you have prioritized the things that you can protect, let's look at some strategies for protecting them.

Life insurance

What does life insurance really protect?

It protects your family's current and future lifestyle. It is the basic protection from financial loss for your loved ones due to an income earner's death. It can ensure that the dreams you had when you were alive don't die with you and can ensure your kids get to stay in the home they currently live in, the school they currently attend, continue the activities they currently enjoy, and attend a college of their choice. It can put your spouse in a strong financial position to not have to remarry someone out of necessity for money.

Through the years, I have heard many statements about life insurance. Some are the most loving and generous and some have been the height of selfishness. A common and wise thought is "What is the probability of actually using life insurance?" Well, 100% of us will die … That is, until Jesus returns.

However, there is no way to know the probability that you will die prematurely. Therefore, ask yourself what would you want to happen if you did die early? Then you can work that answer into your financial plan, of which life insurance and estate planning are a part of.

There is a point when you may decide that you no longer need life insurance. As we age, our financial responsibilities to others typically lessens. I know some grandparents that don't feel that way. But typically, this is true. While your wisdom and experience is needed, you hope that your children grow up and are able to take care of themselves and their own families. It is around this point that we do not need as much life insurance, unless it is for large estate planning needs.

Therefore, how much life insurance and the type that we purchase matters. There are many different opinions out there about how much life insurance one should purchase. It is imperative that you don't fall victim to following a generalized rule when doing any type of planning especially regarding the future financial security of your family or business.

These are factors to consider when calculating your insurance needs and wants:

- Your current income

- Your current age

- Number of dependents

- The cost of the policy in relation to your budget
- How long you will need the policy
- The income earning capacity of your spouse or dependents
- Your current assets
- Your debt
- Future financial costs such as college, weddings, retirement, and health care
- Your family's willingness and ability to financially help care for those you leave behind
- Funeral costs
- Interest rates and investment returns that you can reliably count on to generate income of the death benefit your beneficiaries receive

You can see how many of these factors can change over time and should be reviewed at least annually or when life events occur such as:

- Divorce
- The birth or adoption of a child
- Retirement
- When you change jobs
- When kids go to college
- When kids graduate college
- When you inherit money
- When you buy a new home
- If you become disabled
- Death of a family member

Regarding the type of life insurance, there are two main types: permanent and term insurance.

Permanent insurance comes in five different types: universal life, whole life, index life, survivorship (second to die), and variable universal life.

Term insurance comes in different lengths of time the insurance is in place. You can lock in the price of the insurance for time periods of anywhere from one year, five years, ten years, to even thirty-five years.

Term insurance is usually used for short-term needs and has a lower cost than permanent insurance and is a great option if you are trying to fit the premium into your budget. However, be aware that term insurance is not designed to keep over the long haul.

There are advantages and disadvantages to each of these. They were all designed for a purpose. This is when your holistic plan is valuable. You must know what problems you are solving for and what risk that you want insured. None of us want to be "sold" life insurance. But we want a potential problem solved. Life insurance is an emotional purchase. It logically does not benefit the insured person. But it provides for those that we love when they cannot do so themselves. Old life insurance policies once included the verse James 1:27 (ESV) "Religion that is pure and undefiled before God the Father is this: to visit orphans and widows in their affliction…" To visit meant to care for orphans and widows; life insurance is designed for us to provide for those we love if we do orphan them.

SICKNESS OR INJURY

There are clearly other risks in life that do not include you dying. We all have the risk of illness leading to high medical costs. In fact, this can be back breaking financially. We can also be disabled and no longer able to earn an income. This section, in fact the entire chapter, is not meant to be so morbid. Yet we must look at these risks, plan for them, and live life trusting God as we discussed earlier in the book.

Health, disability, and long-term care insurance can protect your assets and cash flow from a sickness, illness, or long-term injury. Property and casualty insurance that covers your home, auto, and other property is designed to protect those assets in a way that if or when they are damaged then the insurance pays for the repair or replacement of that property.

Many people think the biggest asset they have is their home or their retirement account; however, during your working years your ability to earn income is by far your greatest asset. If your income stops due to an injury or illness, your ability to fund your current responsibilities, obligations, and future plans will be derailed. Therefore, protecting your income is a significant part of your financial plan.

Libraries of books have been written on insurance. Your financial advisor should walk you through this process or seek an insurance professional to help.

Continue to think about insurance as a form of risk management for your financial plan. As your plan evolves, you can save money on insurance premiums if you have the available cash to have a higher deductible plan. You can also pay a higher premium and purchase a lower deductible plan with maybe even more features. However, I continue to stress that you must know of the potential problems that you are solving for. This will help you be an educated buyer of the insurances that you seek.

"WISE PEOPLE DON'T ATTEMPT TO PREDICT THE FUTURE; THEY PREPARE FOR IT."

—DAVE JESIOLOWSKI

CHAPTER 9

ESTATE PLANNING AND END OF LIFE PLANNING

"MONEY CHANGES PEOPLE. THEREFORE, YOU WANT IT TO CHANGE YOUR FAMILY IN A POSITIVE WAY AND NOT A DETRIMENTAL WAY."

—RALPH YELVERTON

At one time, estate planning was primarily for tax purposes and it was everyone's trigger. In recent years, the tax code has changed raising the estate tax phase out or exemption level above $11 million per person. Therefore, tax preparation is no longer the top consideration in estate planning for the average person. However, there is far more involved. We think of estate planning as a key piece in a financial plan. You have responsibilities that surpass your death that insurance alone cannot solve for. Therefore, estate planning is used for family legacy planning and protection; care for disabled and/or minor family members; and end of life care, decision making, and planning.

I have a precious client that is a dear old friend. Very early in my career I taught a money management class at church. This sweet older lady attended. She was attentive and eager to learn, even after she already had a successful financial plan in place. She owned land that had been in her family for generations. Now the city was building a minor highway as a major bypass directly through the middle of this land. The value of this great old farm and hunting land grew by a decimal place in just a few years. She and I had a conversation about this. It was apparent that she and her family now had an estate tax issue. In fact, if she had passed away at that time, her family would have had to sell at least half of the land at "fire sale prices" just to pay the taxes. In this conversation, she looked at me and in the sweetest voice said, "But Chris, I don't want to be rich."

I replied, "But the IRS says that you are …"

As a result of this, she and her family met with attorneys, planned well, and stayed focused. Now, many years later, her entire financial plan is still in good shape even after many life changes.

The purpose of your estate plan is the orderly transition of your assets to those that you love. As for end of life planning, you have a responsibility to yourself to make as many decisions as possible and put them in writing so they can be carried out.

For this chapter, our purpose is to outline possible pieces to your plan. In this context, it is impossible to give advice directly to you. Therefore, our goal is to educate you in a way to help you learn more.

WHAT ARE THE FOUNDATIONAL TOOLS OF ESTATE PLANNING?

Will: Also called a last will and testament. It is a document describing what you want to happen to your estate when you die. In a will, you name your heirs, a guardian for your minor children, and also an executor for your will (the person to collect and distribute your assets). However, a will is only enforceable if it complies with the probate laws of your state. [5]

You can use your will to ensure that your assets are distributed the way you want them to be after your death. If you don't have a will, the state that you live in has a legal process to give the ownership of your assets to those the state considers your heirs. For most of us, we would rather decide that for ourselves.

In this process your estate will go to probate. This is not the scary process that some think that it is. But it can be frustrating, especially if the person that has passed away does not have a will. Probate is the legal process of ensuring that all creditors are paid and that ownership of all assets are legally transferred. This is one of those unique areas of our legal system that help give our assets value and ensures those values are recognized.

Power of Attorney for Health Care: A Health Care Power of Attorney (HCPOA) is a legal document that allows an individual to designate another person to make medical decisions for him or her when he or she cannot make decisions for himself or herself. Health care decisions include the power to consent, refuse consent, or withdraw consent to any type of medical care, treatment, service, or procedure. A HCPOA is also referred to as health care proxy, medical power of attorney, and Durable Power of Attorney for Health Care. [6]

When used in real life, this can give great comfort to those making medical decisions for someone else. This allows you to choose someone that you respect to make your health decisions if you cannot. You can also give them guidance, such as a "do not resuscitate" clause or what to do if you are on life support, among others. This gives the person that you have chosen confidence as they deal with a potentially difficult and emotional situation.

Power of Attorney for Assets: Power of attorney of property is a legal document transferring the legal right to the attorney or agent to manage and access the principal's property in the event the principal is unable to do so themselves. [7]

When these are enacted properly, they can facilitate a smoothness of managing assets when that smoothness is absolutely needed. A person can use these anytime they want someone else to act on their behalf. The scope of that action can be as broad or as limited as you choose. In my experience, these have been used when a person can no longer make decisions for themselves. In this case, a court can appoint a guardian for you. However, this is a difficult time to make that happen. Having a Power of Attorney can help your family focus on you in a time of health crisis and not have to visit with attorneys, judges, and financial advisors.

Trust: A trust is a fiduciary relationship in which one party, known as a trustor, gives another party, the trustee, the right to hold title to property or assets for the benefit of a third party, the beneficiary. Trusts are established to provide legal protection for the trustor's assets, to make sure those assets are distributed according to the wishes of the trustor, and to save time, reduce paperwork and, in some cases, avoid or reduce inheritance or estate taxes. [8]

Trusts work like an entity that is set up to hold your assets for someone else. These tools are used broadly for asset protection from creditors and wayward in-laws. These are used for financial longevity in charities and ministries. Trusts can be used to hold assets for young children until they mature. These can also be used in multiple end of life planning scenarios. There is a time and a place for these tools. I often hear someone say I need to set up a trust for XYZ, when in reality that have a specific outcome in mind and they have heard that a trust can do that. The best advice is to meet with an attorney that you trust, outline the outcome you want, and ask for their advice.

WHAT ARE SOME OF THE ISSUES THAT YOU SHOULD BE MINDFUL OF?

Lifetime Gifting: If you are gifting assets away to family members, be mindful there are rules that could affect you. In 2019, any gift(s) valued over $15,000, may result in taxes being owed. Generally, the donor pays this tax. These can be combined with a spouse so that a couple can gift $30,000 in 2019 without taxes being owed.

Business Succession: For successful business owners, their business is often their most valuable asset. However, I have seen many business owners not manage the equity in their business as such or even know their business value. We do a great job of thinking, planning, and growing our businesses. Then we don't manage the equity and plan our exit. This really does not make good business sense, but it makes all of the human sense in the world. Please don't make this mistake. There is no magic formula for managing a business succession. Yet there are a few formulas that fit. Whether you are selling to family members, younger partners that you've mentored, or on the open market, manage the equity with diligence. In my experience, businesses that manage their equity are better run than those that don't. Consider starting years in advance.

Disabled family members: This is both an emotional and a logical topic. You may have a family member that cannot care for themselves. Maybe they were born disabled, an illness or age has caused this, or a tragedy left them impaired. Regardless, years of care and your heart for them has made this topic near and dear to you. Logically, you are in the best position to know what this person needs. Now, you must consider who will take care of them if or when you cannot. This is not a topic that we can fully unpack in the scope of this chapter. However, you should spend time thinking about and researching what this person needs and what resources are available to them. Then meet with your financial advisor and/or an attorney to lay out what needs to take place for this person to be cared for if you are not available to provide that care. This is an area where a trust becomes a valuable and often utilized tool.

Minor children: Parents pay attention, especially those with young children. This also applies to anyone with guardianship of a young child. You have a tremendous responsibility. If you and your spouse die prematurely, who will take care of your children and how? This is an important decision. First, think about who. Do their morals and thoughts regarding raising children closely align with yours? Are they financially able? Are you leaving them money to do so? You should if you can. Who is managing this money? These questions and others should be explored privately and then with an advisor. Next, since you are leaving money for the children, when will they get it? If you are well prepared with a solid financial plan with growing investments and are properly insured (which after this book it is our hope that you are!), you may leave your young children a large amount of money.

If this is left when they are very young and invested with years of growth, this amount could grow very large. I don't know about you, but the last thing that I needed at eighteen years old, which is the age of inheritance in most states, was a lot of money for me to blow on all of the stupid things that a rich eighteen-year-old can find. Therefore, within your financial plan, consider carefully who would raise your children and how you will provide for that.

Also consider how and when your young children would receive their inheritance. Again, a trust is a tool that can be used to manage assets for your young children and dictate the terms by which they receive that inheritance. As they age, take this topic as one of many opportunities to teach them excellent money management so they grow up financially prepared.

"*A good man leaves an inheritance to his children's children.*" Proverbs 13:22 (ESV) This is such a powerful verse and one you will think about one day. At the end of your life, you will wonder, *Am I leaving a good inheritance?* First and foremost, this has nothing to do with money. You should leave a family legacy of love for God and people. Teach your family to do what is right, to love, to be kind, and walk humbly with Christ. Teach them to work hard and seek wisdom. Then if you can leave them a financial inheritance, certainly do so. This is an excellent gift, along with the inheritance that you plan for them, as it teaches them how to manage their money wisely and be generous. This is something that wealthy families do very well. They often leave a legacy of financial wisdom.

Jonathan Edwards was a powerful Godly minister during the Great Awakening in the Thirteen Colonies during the 1730s and 1740s. He was one of the Puritans that John Piper calls "Redwoods of the Christian faith." His family legacy is a great example for us. Edwards was a Godly man, hardworking, intelligent, and moral. It is written that he poured love into his family, talked and listened, and taught and prayed with them. One hundred and fifty years after his death, his lineage was studied. His descendants include: one US vice president, one dean of a law school, one dean of a medical school, three

US senators, three governors, three mayors, thirteen college presidents, thirty judges, sixty doctors, sixty-five professors, seventy-five military officers, eighty public office holders, one hundred lawyers, one hundred clergymen, and two hundred eighty-five college graduates. Certainly, our family bloodline may not hold this pedigree in 150 years, but **all of us can leave a legacy of love, encouragement, and wisdom.** The truth is a few generations from now, no one will remember your name. A few possibly might, but most likely not. This may sound depressing, but it is simply true. However, **you can love, encourage, and shape your children and grandchildren. You can point them to the truth of Christ, teach them to love others, and live fulfilled.** They, in turn, will teach their children, and their children for generations to come. **This is a powerful family legacy that has value and purpose.** [9]

"A GOOD MAN LEAVES AN INHERITANCE TO HIS CHILDREN'S CHILDREN…"

—PROVERBS 13:22 (ESV)

CHAPTER 10

TAXES

Thanks, Mr. Franklin, for this famous saying of certainty. Taxes can be so frustrating, especially if you don't like how your tax dollars are being spent. Yet consider how safe and stable our nation really is. Our governments—national, state, and local—are well-funded and stable entities when compared to the rest of the world. Our taxes are the price that we pay to live in a stable society.

Now this is not meant to sound like the beginning of an incendiary blog post. I respect your opinion on this matter. Regardless of our feelings, we all have to pay taxes. This is an important responsibility and a costly one if you get wrong.

Therefore, let's start on the right foot. For this section, we will keep things simple. You can google tax tips until your fingertips bruise. But these are a few important thoughts as an individual: what taxes apply to you?

In regards to your financial plan, income taxes and capital gains taxes are your main taxes. Federal taxes typically are the largest amount and the focus of attention. As an employee, you fill out a W-4 stating your marriage status and deductions or you can state a flat amount to withhold. This sets up the dollar figure withheld from your payroll and remitted to the IRS and state governments on your behalf. There is not a lot of creativity in this. Simply state the correct amount or your best estimate. The IRS is a terrible lender and borrower of money, so your best option is typically to pay them what you owe them on time. Nothing more, nothing less.

As an employee, you have a few options to lower your current taxes. Typically, your best options are employer-sponsored retirement plans such as 401(k), 403(b), SEP, and SIMPLE IRA. These are investment options that allow you to invest pre- or post-tax into traditional plans and many now offer Roth options.

The traditional qualified plan allows you to invest pre-tax and roll over your investments into a traditional IRA after age 59 ½ or at retirement. In the traditional option, you will pay income taxes on your IRA distributions, which are required to start by at least age 70 ½. This is the most commonly used retirement investment income today. The Roth option allows you to invest post-tax and roll your investments over into a Roth IRA at retirement. You can then take an income tax free. There are tremendous tax advantages to both options. They can grow tax deferred or tax free, potentially for decades, which can be very valuable financially. The traditional option gives you a tremendous tax benefit today while the Roth option gives you a tremendous tax benefit in the future. The question of which one is best for you typically depends on your tax state laws. The younger you are, the further away from retirement, and the less predictable the applicable tax laws are the more you want to balance between these two options if they are available to you. Which is better for you and what is the best balance is a clear question to be answered in a financial planning process.

Also within your investment plans you may find passive income that is taxable. Of course, this is not just "found" but invested in and earned over time. Passive income may come from investments in non-retirement accounts holding stocks, bonds, or packaged products like mutual funds, real estate, business investments, or a plethora of ideas. Passive income or unearned income is often described as income that does not require work. The federal tax rate on this income varies from one type to another. For example, interest income from your savings account is taxed as ordinary income. Stock dividends have two categories—ordinary and qualified—depending on how long you have held the stock. Capital gains are gains from selling an asset like a stock or a mutual fund. Short-term capital gains are gains from an asset that you have held for a year or less. These are taxed at your ordinary income tax rate, while long-term gains have a different tax rate of 0%, 15%, or 20%.

All of these taxes are reported on your tax filings that are required, along with any payment owed, by April 15 of each year. Or you can file an extension. Of course, much of this information is known and there is a lot of opportunity for taking care of these actions yourself. It is not our purpose to get complicated on these matters. However, they can get complicated quickly on their own.

So how do you get all of this done? Our team recommends that you use a CPA if your taxes get the least bit complicated. Stay organized, keep important information throughout the year. There is a lot of technology that can help with this, so ask your financial advisor or CPA. Be on time and engaged when it is time to file your taxes. This is an easy topic to ignore and overlook.

When using a CPA, they can and should become a trusted advisor. In fact, this is true for your financial advisor and attorney. **Surrounding yourself with good advisors is imperative. Your advisors can help you be profitable, purposeful, and give you expertise in areas that would**

take you a career to learn. So get to know them and interview them. Find out if you are like-hearted and like-minded. Can they give you advice that aligns with your morals and ideas? Will they admit when they don't know or when they are wrong? Go work and research to find the right answer. Will they disagree with you when they should and stand their ground? Having an advisor that will do this for you is extremely valuable.

I realize that we get frustrated with taxes. It is no fun to give your money to an entity for them to do something that you may or may not agree with. However, as stated earlier, it is one cost to live in a stable society with a healthy and complete infrastructure.

In closing, the following is a story from a good friend. He is a missionary in a third-world country, far away in a dangerous place. He is also a client and had capital gains taxes to pay. After an email discussion regarding his taxes, this was his response:

"It's a rich man's problem. Compared to how most of the world survives from day-to-day, we will be okay. I was reminded of that last week when I took a pair of shoes to a guy to be repaired. His name is John. His shop is located on the sidewalk where he sits all day repairing shoes. He is crippled and has very little in the way of material goods but has a heart of gold. He wanted to charge me $0.50 for fixing the shoes. I paid him significantly more and had a good gospel conversation."

This puts our "rich man's" problems into perspective . . .

"THE HARDEST THING IN THE WORLD TO UNDERSTAND
IS THE INCOME TAX."

—ALBERT EINSTEIN

CHAPTER 11

WHO CAN YOU TRUST?

"TRUST, BUT VERIFY."

—RONALD REAGAN, 40TH PRESIDENT OF THE UNITED STATES

It is fitting to include a short chapter on advisors. Most of us are not trained in how to use advisors. I still remember some of the best advice I ever received on this topic. Our firm was interviewing marketing consulting firms for a large project in which we were working with a group of firms nationwide. My background was in sales and I thought that I knew marketing. As I talked to a friend, I told him what I thought we should accomplish and asked him questions on how to get this done. He told me, "Chris, stop trying to prove how much you know. These consultants work for you. Let them prove to you how much they know!" This was great advice and resonated with me in my own career. Our job, as advisors, is to serve *you*, the client. You don't have to be an expert, because you have hired us to be that for you.

"Can I trust you?" This is the first question that you should ask. Can you trust the advisor's integrity and competence? **Are they honest? Are they capable?** Will they do what they say they will do? *Can* they do what they say they will do?

The challenge many investors have today is finding a person that they can trust to give them unbiased guidance and direction on their financial plans without trying to sell them something that is self serving.

An advisor that is simply a salesman can do you more harm than good. This is true in any profession, whether they are a doctor, an attorney, a CPA, a stockbroker, an insurance agent, or any other professional that is simply selling you their service. However, it can be as detrimental to you if you try to accomplish any of these tasks mentioned yourself. For example, have you ever known anyone who diagnosed their own heart condition? You may answer yes. But how did that turn out for them?

Typically, we visit a doctor when we need one. The same is true for a CPA or an attorney. However, the challenge is that most people don't know which professionals are available to work with, when to work with one, or how to work with a professional in a way that you get the best from them.

So what should an advisor do for you? Just like a doctor should first listen, a professional advisor should *listen* to you and your needs. Prescription without diagnosis is malpractice. This is true in the legal, tax, and financial realm. But we will focus on ten areas that your financial advisor should discuss with you first. These ten are based on a study by Envestnet and the book *The Essential Advisor* by William C. Crager and Jay Hummel.

1. Identifies your needs (dreams, goals, targets).

2. Puts your goals first.

3. Helps you understand your financial plan by cutting through the noise of the market.

4. Works to understand your personal circumstances, values, investing style, tax situation, and goals.

5. Develops and carefully monitors a personal plan for you; makes timely portfolio adjustments to meet your changing needs.

6. Helps you understand fees and expenses and the value added from these fees.

7. Responds with true care and concern when you are faced with life transitions.

8. Has tailored communication, education, and experience to meet your unique needs and concerns.

9. Communicates clearly, truthfully, and consistently.

10. Effectively utilizes technology to maximize time.

When you are investing your money and you have hired someone to do a job, hold them accountable to these standards. The right advisor will appreciate this and you will get a great effort from them.

The relationship is key. In our fast-paced world, the word *relationship* is so watered down with social media definitions and fewer opportunities for personal contact. So build a relationship with the professionals that you call your advisors while expecting a high level of expertise. You'll be glad that you did.

So how can you quantify this? It is hard, at times, to say "this advisor" is worth this much money in return to me. If return on your money is all that you want, then be clear with your advisor. Then hold on because you may be invested very aggressively. This may not be the best for you. Succeeding at your dreams, goals, and targets are what you really want. As we have discussed throughout the book, don't use money as a scoreboard! Measure your plans, be focused and disciplined, and expect your advisor to be as well. Judge your success with your advisors against your goals and the role they play. After all, **your success in your plans is your responsibility.**

So how can you quantify their value? A study by Envestnet[10] demonstrated that a financial advisor, properly doing their job, can be worth up to 3% in return for you. This is not including full asset management–produced returns as those could be too vague to argue "who" produced those returns.

These are the five areas that your advisor should work for you and be able to educate you.

Financial planning: Your advisor should develop a plan with you to achieve your dreams, goals, and targets. They should be your expert, working with you as a business partner for your success.

Asset allocation: Your advisor should input your needs first and should understand your goals and the risk that you are willing to take to achieve those goals. Risk in this case is the risk of market loss to earn market-produced gains. The advisor should have a solid investment philosophy, policy, and procedures that are a roadmap to build a portfolio for you.

Investment selection: The selection of the investment positions used in your portfolio should be diverse, tested, and fit within an investment philosophy that can reasonably be expected to deliver the results that you desire.

Systematic rebalancing: Your investment portfolio should be periodically rebalanced so that your investments stay within the ranges that were originally built. This means that periodically, some positions need to be sold and others bought to realign your portfolio.

The decision-making process asset allocation, investment selection, and systematic rebalancing should be rules-based and predictable. You want a portfolio whereby the process to build your portfolio can be explained to you, not sold to you. We believe the best method of building a portfolio is with a rules-based decision-making process that is tested before it is implemented. Then it is predictable and repeatable in the future. When I say predictable, I do not mean the portfolio's returns will be predictable, but that your decision making is predictable, so that the returns can be projected based on past results. You can then build your financial plan with these returns projections and know your process (or your advisor's process) to make future decisions when future events happen.

Tax management: By incorporating strategies such as tax loss harvesting, a good advisor can save you basis points in tax areas that add up over time. This is tedious work that requires your financial advisor and tax advisor working together.

As you think about the advisors in your life, get to know them and let them get to know you. Know your dreams and maybe your goals, then don't be afraid to let them craft other goals and targets with you. This is their job. Then as trust grows over time, don't judge them by returns only just because "everybody else does." Judge them by the total package they deliver to you.

CHAPTER 12
PLANNED GENEROSITY

"IN 1974, WE ENDED UP WITH A FAMINE IN THE COUNTRY. PEOPLE WERE DYING OF HUNGER AND NOT HAVING ENOUGH TO EAT. AND THAT'S A TERRIBLE SITUATION TO SEE AROUND YOU. AND I WAS FEELING TERRIBLE THAT HERE I TEACH ELEGANT THEORIES OF ECONOMICS, AND THOSE THEORIES ARE OF NO USE AT THE MOMENT WITH THE PEOPLE WHO ARE GOING HUNGRY. SO I WANTED TO SEE IF AS A PERSON, AS A HUMAN BEING, I COULD BE OF SOME USE TO SOME PEOPLE . . . I THOUGHT THAT IF YOU CAN BECOME AN ANGEL FOR $27, IT WOULD BE FUN TO DO MORE OF IT."

—DR. MUHAMMAD YUNUS, GRAMEEN BANK

Dr. Yunus was born in India in 1940. Educated in economics, he earned the opportunity to work in the US in 1969. With a PhD from Vanderbilt, a college professorship, and a brilliant mind, Yunus was set to succeed in the world of economics and finance. Of course, in America, this meant the possibility of growing tremendous wealth.

Yet Dr. Yunus thought differently than most or maybe he just acted on his thoughts. He chose to return home after the Bangladesh Liberation War in 1971, in which he had raised support in the US. Once a leader in the government's planning commission and then an economics professor, he could see the poverty all around him. A famine in

1974 opened his eyes to the widespread destruction that poverty can cause. He chose to do something.

In the mid-1970s, Dr. Yunus experimented with lending $27 to forty-two women in the village of Jobra near the university in which he taught in Chittagong. Banks of that day would not lend to the poor because of default rates and lack of collateral—similar to today. The loan sharks on the streets charged extortionate rates as they were the only option. His microlending ideas and actions were a success. He expanded these both academically and in practice, establishing Grameen Bank. This bank has grown globally with currently 9 million members and over 2,500 locations having loaned over $26 billion since its inception. Ninety-seven percent of the members are women. "They own the bank. It is a bank owned by poor women," Dr. Yunus said in 2017. "The repayment rate is 99.6%." [11][12]

One person with a passion to make a difference and a willingness to invest their money, time, and resources can make a major impact on people's lives.

Each of us have an innate, God-given desire to be purposeful in our lives. In nearly every area of our life we are searching for fulfillment. In entertainment we identify with or escape into what thrills or completes us. With our health, we either strive to get into increasingly better shape or we regularly fulfill pleasure with our bodies—whether that is food, sex, or something else. In work, we strive incessantly for success or our work provides the income to fulfill other desires in our lives. Striving to be purposeful is unavoidable. It is how we are wired. We will seek purpose and fulfillment even if it is our explicit intent not to.

Sadly, most of us seek purpose in the wrong places. Just like an adrenaline-junkie teenager getting drunk because he's bored, we numb our purpose with cheap trinkets and entertainment when God has so much more designed for our life. We are built to seek purpose, to seek fulfillment.

Imagine the greatness of this design. Think globally. There are rich and poor scattered throughout the world. In each area of the world, there are both rich and poor. In some areas there is a large wealth gap. In other areas, there is more of a level playing field with at least equal opportunity, if not income equality. The rich in some places would be poor in others. Likewise, the poor in certain areas of the world would be rich in others. For example, if you earn $21,000 annually with a household of three, you are on the poverty line in the United States. However, you are in the top 3.2% for per-person income in the world. (For these readers, I realize that you don't feel that way and pray that this book is helping you). With a $32,400 annual income, you will earn your way into the now famous top 1% globally. Let these statistics sink in. *The average income in the US ($59,000) is the top .20% income bracket in the entire world.* [13]

Continue to imagine a design where we all have a desire to be purposeful and fulfilled; a design where we all have an authentic purpose that was not found in more trinkets and false entertainment. **Imagine if this design was carried out, then those of us who were blessed with more would find action in our purpose by sharing with those who need it most.** But how would we share in this design? Would we simply give money away to make ourselves feel better? When we do this, we create a welfare-like mess through charity. Rather, shouldn't we use our resources, time, and skills along with our money to help others in the areas that excite us most? I think this is it. **God has designed us to be excited in certain areas and each of those are different. He has designed us to be purposeful with our resources, time, skills, and money in those areas of excitement. We will find our fulfillment in Him, and the actions that are a part of this**

fulfillment through being purposeful are what we are blessed with.

Therefore, the choice is yours of where to direct your purposeful desires. Do you direct it inwardly, working harder and harder to earn more profit to buy more pleasures? We all know that more stuff will not satisfy our desires. More trips, more trinkets, and more trophies will just lead to us building larger trophy cases to house our stuff to collect dust. Earning more and more just leads to more of the same thing that you have today. Should you or could you instead focus your desire for value outwardly to serve others? You could start collecting skills, growing in knowledge and wisdom, and garnering resources to serve others. You could start earning more and more so that you can give more away. Are these two desires in conflict?

Yes and no. Just like you were designed to be purposeful, you were designed to be profitable. You should work hard, invest, and strive to earn. Think, plan, and grow to be a great success. We are blessed to be in a place in the world with great opportunity. You have access to opportunities, education, and resources that most people globally cannot even dream about. These are blessings to you for you to use and excel with. But **"much is required from those to whom much is given, for their responsibility is greater."** [14] Profit is not the end purpose, it is only a part of the means to the end. It is simply a tool. You are needed greatly. Your skills, time, resources, and yes, your money, are needed. You need to be purposeful and others need you to be purposeful on their behalf. This is no accident. See the greatness in this design. God has blessed us with resources, built us with a desire to be purposeful, and there is a world in need of us to do so.

Before we go the wrong direction theologically, let's look at a few truths. You can be someone's friend and generous benefactor, but not their Savior. It is through Jesus Christ that anyone is actually saved or rescued from their failures and shame. In our role of being purposeful, we are serving others and giving God the honor for this. He is the origin of our blessings. It is His design that allows us to be a part of His plans. If you find *all* of your fulfillment in being purposeful, it too will become as nasty of a monster in your life as finding all of your fulfillment in earning more and more money. Next, don't see the brokenness of the needs in the world as a part of God's original design. This will lead us to a wrong understanding of God's sovereignty and plans. In Romans 8:28 (ESV), Paul writes that *"for those who love God all things work together for good, for those who are called according to His purpose."* This is pointing to God taking the brokenness in this world, the evil and the misery, and redeeming this for His glory and His people's good. Neither of these truths make sense if we are looking through our own lens. We simply aren't big enough. However, you cannot deny the greatness of this design. Even in a broken world, which no one will argue that it's not broken, there is a solution. Yet that solution cannot come solely from human design because we are not capable of that. It is clear that we are to participate in the solution. All the while, we do not create a welfare state. All of us participate locally and worldwide. Lastly, we should not view our profit as a bargaining chip with God. We don't co-op God for personal gain. We that are blessed enjoy our blessings, but those don't rule us. We become purposeful and fulfilled. Our blessing becomes tools. Our success becomes a part of our purpose, but not our identity. We find our identity in Christ and the rest falls into place.

Let's look at a classic old story that Jesus once told. In the parable of The Good Samaritan, we can imagine that the Samaritan was a businessman, traveling to the city of Jericho. They walked a route that was rocky, narrow, and dangerous. A traveler was attacked, beaten, robbed, and left for dead. Two men passed the near-dead man, both of whom we could assume should help him. These passersby were a priest and a Levite, both members of the Jewish religion. On this road, we could speculate that these men would have had to nearly step over the traveler's body to avoid him. Both men were blessed with the resources to help and both chose not to. Then the Samaritan passed by. In the time of this story, there was religious and racist bigotry between Jews and Samaritans. Considering that the audience of Jesus' story was Jewish, no one would have expected the Samaritan to help the traveler. In fact, it would be shocking that he did. Yet the Samaritan felt compassion for the traveler. He cleaned the blood from the man's body, disinfected the dirt from the wounds, and did his best to soothe the man's pain. He put him on his own donkey and walked the rest of the way to Jericho. The Samaritan spent his time, effort, and risked his own life to help this man. Once he arrived in Jericho, he spent his money and his resources. He paid for a hotel room and the physical care of the traveler. The Samaritan told the innkeeper, "Take care of him and whatever more that you spend, when I return I will repay you." In his compassion, the Samaritan cared for another human. Had he not profited financially in his life, if he did not have a few first aid skills, if he was not well traveled, the Samaritan would not have been able to do anything for this man. But he did not dwell on that. He had compassion and used his time, money, and resources to help a person that was in desperate need. As Jesus told this story, He ties it to the command of loving God and loving people. This is our design to *"love God with all of your heart, soul, strength, and mind, and to love your neighbor as yourself."* [15]

How do we do this today? Your money, assets, and profit are your own, a gift from God. What you do with this profit is your responsibility. You are free to choose. The most accurate and freeing viewpoint would be to see ourselves as stewards of this profit. There is an action step that we call planned generosity. This is the intentional planned action to give your money, time, and resources to people in areas that excite you. In your financial plan, you would place tithing and charitable donations as the first amount of money that you give. In fact, if you are a Christian, the Bible is very clear that you should give 10% of your gross income to your church. If you are still undecided in this area but you want to be intentional about giving or you plan an offering beyond your tithe, then think about what areas of society, locally or worldwide, where you want to effect change. Plan specifically to give a portion of your resources. Spend time working with this organization. Get to know them and those they serve. Go work humbly but with confidence that you have something to bring. Do not be arrogant because you are showing up with a checkbook. Being the "money man" and dictating how things get done is destructive. But go to work in the areas that excite you, have compassion like the Good Samaritan, and bring your best.

We view planned generosity as a part of being both profitable and purposeful. This is a God-given task, adventure, and privilege in our daily lives. In 2 Corinthians 9:10–11 (TLB), Paul writes that *"For God, who gives seed to the farmer to plant, and later on good crops to harvest and eat, will give you more and more seed to plant and will make it grow so that you can give away more and more fruit from your harvest. Yes, God will give you much so that you can give away much, and when we take your gifts to those who need them they will break out into thanksgiving and praise to God for your help."*

This writing is clear. God provides opportunities, education, and resources for you to profit. As a part of His blessing you should enjoy some of your profit, thanking Him for your blessings. As a part of this action, you should be generous and cheerfully give to others. This planned generosity will be a part of you fulfilling your purpose in this life.

So ask yourself: if you were to gain more money, that next promotion, or the next level of wealth, **would that fulfill you?**

If not, what would? **What do you think you're missing?**

How do you plan to respond to the needs in the world and your need to be intentional in giving your time, money, and resources to others?

Where do you want to give? What excites you?

Spend time thinking and praying about your opportunities to give. Ask God to excite you, to give you opportunities and courage. Then go and give!

ENDNOTES

1   "TIAA-CREF Survey finds Americans spend less time planning their IRA investment than choosing a restaurant," TIAA, March 13, 2014, https://www.tiaa.org/public/about-tiaa/news-press/press-releases/pressrelease495.html

2   "S&P 500 Total Returns," https://www.slickcharts.com/sp500/returns

3   Quotation plus the following pages are from *Invest to Prosper* by Clint W. Sorenson, pages 67-73.

4   "Is Tiger Woods Loss Averse? Persistent Bias in the Face of Experience, Competition, and High Stakes," Devin G. Pope, Maurice E. Scheweitzer, *American Economic Review*, Issue 101 (February 2011), pp. 129–157, https://www.aeaweb.org/articles?id=10.1257/aer.101.1.129

5   "Definition of a Legal Will," Teo Spengler, https://info.legalzoom.com/definition-legal-will-4222.html

6   "Health Care Power Of Attorney Law and Legal Definition," UsLegal, https://definitions.uslegal.com/h/health-care-power-of-attorney/

7   "Power of Attorney of Property," Will Kenton, updated May 30, 2018, https://www.investopedia.com/terms/p/powerofattorneyproperty.asp

8   "Trust," Julia Kagan, updated May 5, 2019, https://www.investopedia.com/terms/t/trust.asp

9   "Multigenerational Legacies — The Story of Jonathan Edwards," Larry Ballard, July 1, 2017, https://www.ywam-fmi.org/news/multigenerational-legacies-the-story-of-jonathan-edwards/

10   https://www.envestnet.com/essentialadvisor

11 "'We are all entrepreneurs': Muhammad Yunus on the changing the world, one microloan at a time," *The Guardian*, published March 28, 2017, https://www.theguardian.com/sustainable-business/2017/mar/29/we-are-all-entrepreneurs-muhammad-yunus-on-changing-the-world-one-microloan-at-a-time

12 Grameen Bank January 2019 month report, published February 9, 2019, http://www.grameen-info.org/monthly-reports-01-2019

13 Global Rich List (website), http://www.globalrichlist.com/. "Are You in the Top One Percent of the World," Daniel Kurt, Investopedia, updated May 9, 2019 https://www.investopedia.com/articles/personal-finance/050615/are-you-top-one-percent-world.asp

14 Luke 12:48; The Bible translation

15 Luke 10:25-37

REFERENCES

Statistical references: Federal Reserve's 2013 Survey of Consumer Finance <u>indicated</u> that median financial assets held by American families are only about $21,000.

Writing in the *American Journal of Family Therapy*, Joan Atwood notes that "couples would prefer to talk about sex or infidelities rather than how they handle family finances or how much money they earn."

"Nielsen: Even Many High Earners Live Paycheck To Paycheck," Ted Knutson, *Financial Advisor*, published August 6, 2015, https://www.fa-mag.com/news/nielsen--even-many-high-earners-live-paycheck-to-paycheck-22704.html

"Most Americans live paycheck to paycheck," Jessica Dickler, CNBC, published August 24, 2017, updated Wednesday August 30, 2017, https://www.cnbc.com/2017/08/24/most-americans-live-paycheck-to-paycheck.html

"An honest look at the personal financial crisis," Elizabeth White, TedxVCU, February 2017, https://www.ted.com/talks/

elizabeth_white_an_honest_look_at_the_personal_finance_crisis/
transcript#t-4424

Recommended Reading

Investments: *Invest to Prosper* by Clint Sorenson and Robert Leggett

Relationships: *The Love Dare* by Stephen Kendrick and Alex Kendrick

Risk: *Thinking Fast and Slow* by Daniel Kahneman

Decision Making: *One Decision Can* by Dave Jesiolowski

Spiritual Purpose (& generally all of life & eternity!): The Bible

About Chris

With over a decade and a half of helping clients manage their finances and move from a life of work to retirement, Chris has helped his clients align their purpose with their profit in their financial plans. In his current role as managing partner with Sound Financial Strategies, he has been instrumental in crafting a vision of something that is bigger than money. He, along with the Sound  team, have created a culture where people can fulfill their God-given purpose all while working to be profitable. Chris lives out this vision by serving in many capacities from mission trips, to being a deacon at his church, to prison ministries, to volunteering time with Sound's Purpose Partners to help those in need. Chris is passionate about Jesus Christ, a loving husband to Christie, and father to three wonderful amazing girls, Kate, Rachel, and Megan. Born in Mississippi, Chris is passionate about growing Sound Financial, which is headquartered in Jackson, Mississippi. Sound has grown from a small Mississippi firm founded by Sammy Dean and Danny Matthews over two and a half decades ago in 1993 to a firm that now manages the assets for many wonderful people who worked at some of the world's largest corporations.

The vision for Sound Financial Strategies is to reach as many people as possible to help them make better decisions surrounding their finances so that can enjoy their journey through life with peace of mind knowing that they will have the resources to fulfill their true purpose in life.

Free Risk Assessment

At Sound Financial we believe that clients should understand risk so they can set realistic goals that align with their lifestyle. We have seen where misaligned portfolio's can lead to failed expectations and frustration. However when investors understand how much risk they are taking in their portfolios, we find that investors are less frustrated during turbulent times in the market. We use the latest leading scientific theory to objectively pinpoint an investor's risk number so they can make decisions that are aligned with the right amount of risk for them to achieve their financial goals. Find out what your number is today by going to the website below or calling to schedule a complimentary risk assessment.

www.soundfsg.com
877 462 3744